PENGUIN BOOKS
RUDRA

Nilima Chitgopekar teaches history at Jesus and Mary College, Delhi University. She is the author of *Encountering Sivaism: The Deity, the Milieu, the Entourage* (1998) and *The Book of Durga* (2003), and has edited *Invoking Goddesses: Gender Politics in Indian Religion* (2002).

RUDRA

THE IDEA OF SHIVA

Nilima Chitgopekar

PENGUIN BOOKS

An imprint of Penguin Random House

PENGUIN BOOKS

USA | Canada | UK | Ireland | Australia
New Zealand | India | South Africa | China | Singapore

Penguin Books is part of the Penguin Random House group of companies
whose addresses can be found at global.penguinrandomhouse.com

Published by Penguin Random House India Pvt. Ltd
4th Floor, Capital Tower 1, MG Road,
Gurugram 122 002, Haryana, India

Penguin
Random House
India

First published by Penguin Books India 2007

10 9 8 7 6 5 4 3 2

ISBN 9780143103417

Typeset in Venetian 301BT and Dante MT by Eleven Arts, New Delhi
Printed at Repro India Limited

www.penguin.co.in

MIX
Paper from
responsible sources
FSC® C047271

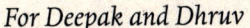

For Deepak and Dhruv

There was so much I wanted to say
but words got in my way

Contents

Introduction

What happens when a concept grabs you and won't let go for decades? What happens when curiosity transforms into an idée fixe?

My fascination with Shiva began with a comfortable, intermittently nonchalant curiosity, moving rapidly towards routine academic involvement, where methodologies and rules need to be tenaciously followed. This ensured that complete absorption was kept at bay—until more recently. There has been disquietude, albeit a pleasant one, as my interest has ultimately advanced to a sustained sense of wonder at the evolution of a god-concept that, like a palimpsest, has come to embody several levels of human existence. In a land where there is a profusion of gods and then some, Shiva is one deity who straddles, in a mythico-embodied form, many of the key signifiers of Indian culture—dance, music, phallicism, yoga, asceticism, Vedanta, and the rich tradition of heterodoxy and acculturation, to name a few. Spanning the esoteric, the psychological, the mundane, the artistic, from the most obvious to the profoundly symbolic—that is Shiva. The evolution of Shiva's godhood may be used to track historical developments, artistic inclinations, and cultural and philosophical leanings in Hindu tradition over the ages.

Shiva: The name conjures up a melange of images. A rapid-fire listing of what we encounter of him in icons and in his popular myths would include some of the following descriptions:

As Rudra-Shiva, he is at once the creator, destroyer and preserver of the universe;

As the linga, he is without gunas, or attributes, yet the phallicized energy of creation;

As Ardhanarishwara, he is the divine androgyne, the combination of Shiva and Shakti, the male and female manifestations of cosmic energy;

As Mahayogi, he is the ultimate renunciant;

As Shankara, he is the householder, with Parvati as his wife, and Skanda and Ganesha as his children;

As Nataraja, he is the lord of dance, where dance signifies so much more than mere creative movement;

As Pashupati, he is the protector of animals and of our souls;

As Vaidyanatha, he is the supreme healer;

As Mahadeva, he is lord of the gods, the mortals and creatures of the underworld;

As Bhairava, he is the terrifying annihilator and his offerings are liquor or hallucinogens.

Admittedly, this is not a comprehensive inventory, but it does aspire, if not to encapsulate, at least to throw light on the non-linear, polysemic, antinomian and mysterious nature of Shiva. This book is an endeavour to unravel the enigma that is Shiva, with a little help from fiction and history. Sometimes it is not enough to know stories; sometimes there is a desire to know more, to see how a critical analysis can not only enrich but also empower one with the immense variety and tolerance found in ways of looking at a religion.

~

The worship of and belief in Shiva appears to have grown like a self-perpetuating organism. In reality, the Shiva we encounter has endured an eventful career of adapting to, accommodating and spawning numerous deities, cults and practices, and blending representations in old and new myths, beliefs, customs and individual longings. Lest this give the impression of a seamless augmentation of Shiva's persona over the centuries, it is important to understand that overt and surreptitious tensions were often present. This is evident in the robust, colourful and sometimes edgy content of the myths. A visual representation of the myths in iconography, generously laden with prodigious symbolism, also instils in the believer a familiarity with paradox as a part of this deity's life. Over the centuries, Shiva's image has in one way or another been enhanced or attenuated to give us the sum total that we encounter today.

As is common in almost every aspect of Hindu religion, Shiva, as a deity and as a concept, has lent himself to various interpretations and representations over the ages. In Hinduism, one of the fundamental notions that needs to be understood and appreciated is that of multiplicity. Not only do varied cults belonging to different regions and discrete phases of history have their own versions of Shaiva myths and iconography, but certain key myths have also been retold according to sectarian predilections in different Puranas. For instance, in the Puranas with Vaishnava leanings it is inevitably Vishnu who is shown in a better light—that is, 'better' according to the social preferences of the time—than any other god in the pantheon. The same applies to Shiva or Devi in the Puranas dedicated to them. So the myths of Sati's dismemberment, for example, or of the samudramanthan in the quest for amrita, are related differently in different Puranas, with the deviations varying from slight to considerable. In this melee no one telling can be isolated as the ultimate or sole repository of the truth about any god; what may be true for one tradition may not be so for another. Many writers, therefore, find it easier and safer to talk about *a* Shiva, exemplified in *one* tradition, instead of writing about Shiva in a general manner, giving rise to countless micro-studies of Shiva.

Within Hinduism there is no stand-alone god. In Shiva's

cosmic life cycles he has episodes and dealings with many gods, goddesses, godlings and other creatures. In this book, Vishnu, Sati, Daksha, Parvati and Ganesha 'speak' about their experience of stepping into Shiva's transformative world. Each voice is followed by an analysis of the encounter as it reflects and is reflected in history and socio-economic proclivities of changing times to suggest a rationale for the profusion of pluralities within the world of Shiva.

This book, then, is also *a* telling of Shiva, but collated from an eclectic set of sources—textual, artistic, inscriptional and oral communication with people who keep themselves involved with Shiva in some way or the other, as dancers, artists, pandits, or believers. Given the sheer abundance of the material at hand, I think it is necessary to outline certain limitations of this somewhat reckless undertaking right at the beginning instead of resorting to an annoying tautology of constant caveats. The retellings of the myths, much of the descriptions, the dialogues between the deities and their states of mind are the product of amalgamating details from various episodes and key myths in Vedic literature and the Puranas. The individual narratives in this book do not strive for accuracy, which, due to the reasons already elaborated, would not only be an impossibility but would also fail to qualify as a virtue. From the many versions of a single episode I have had to 'choose' one, as a genuflection to the flow of narration without annoying and jerky breaks. Given a different genre, there would be no need to give consistency to amorphous, wriggly myths that can so easily alter to fit the demands of a situation.

But the 'demand' this book fulfils is to offer a storyline for Shiva's life that reveals rather than confuses.

~

Sanskrit texts of the brahmanical tradition, deemed as scripture or 'high' religion, are some of the main sources of the myths used in this book. This includes the Vedas, the appended Brahmanas and Upanishads, as well as the Puranas. Chronologically, the Vedas are the most ancient and are often, albeit fallaciously, placed the highest on the totem pole of literary sources for the early history of India. They are used to 'excavate' the foundational ideas of Hinduism and the incipient genealogies of Hindu deities. But this is not entirely correct, for who is to say that other texts did not exist—they may just not have survived—or that other traditions simply did not 'record' their ideas on life and cosmology? Moreover, as a result of interpolations and speculations that took place in epochs separated by centuries, Vedic hymns attribute the same qualities to different divinities whose functions are at variance, making it difficult to establish the primary status of Hindu deities. Before one turns to the Vedas as a historical source, it is therefore important to remember that the Vedic 'texts' were 'shruti', that is, 'revealed' texts, committed to memory by religious virtuosos and thereby preserved over centuries. Harping on the Vedic origins of any religion that emerged reflects a longing for unchanged continuity in certain beliefs. In their favour, it is possible that those who composed the Vedas borrowed at least some of their conceptions from the beliefs of a greater public who did not always worship the gods with the same names. These ideas may not have got recorded in any tradition, but may still have contributed to the eventual image of a deity we encounter in the Puranas and the epics.

Where Shiva is concerned, it is significant that many of the characteristics he has been endowed with over millennia cannot be traced back to early brahmanical literature. These are believed to have been derived from the oral/folk traditions that are today collated by ethnographic studies. As far as the Vedas are concerned, it will be pertinent to point out right away that Shiva is not even referred to by this name in the Vedas; there he is Rudra. Some historians strongly believe that the two are not the same deity, while others maintain that certain features present in the Vedic Rudra are found in the Shiva of the Puranas. Often projected as Rudra-Shiva, the resultant deity exemplifies in this double name the process of assimilation that almost all Hindu deities have gone through in some form or the other.

Although the name 'Shiva' is unknown to the Vedas as a name of Rudra, 'Rudra' is a name used for Shiva today and finds mention in the Shiva sahasranama. The meaning of the word 'shiva' is 'auspicious' or 'propitious' and it was applied to a number of Vedic gods as an adjective. A tribe called 'Shivas' is mentioned once in the Rig Veda, but nothing more is known of it. 'Rudra', though its derivation is disputed, is commonly known to mean 'to roar' or 'to howl'. The two combined seem almost like an oxymoron, since, literally, Rudra-Shiva would come to mean 'benign howler'. Even if we suppose that they were two separate entities who were later merged, my interest would lie in the lineage of thought that has wedded them and I would be driven to seek the characteristics that have insufflated each other to create the composite and hyphenated Rudra-Shiva.

Many aspects of Shiva's Vedic past make him the bête noire among the Hindu gods. In subsequent centuries this allowed him to amass within his being all kinds of heterodox behaviour. One of the most significant elements in the formation of the Hindu Shiva concept from the Rigvedic Rudra is that of the destroyer, feared by gods and humans alike. Although Shiva is usually benign, almost antithetically so when compared to Rudra, we find him manifesting himself in frightening forms such as Bhairava and Virabhadra when his fiercer aspect is required to show itself. Thus, Rudra keeps alive the darker associations which can accommodate the antinomian forms of Shiva and his fierce (ugra) forms. In these forms he seems to threaten not only the individual but also the very fabric of society, much like Kali and Chamunda who emerge from Durga's brow in dire situations.

Hymns in the Rig Veda paint Rudra as a destructive, capricious and frightening god. He is malevolent, the personification of everything that is a menace to the world. Massively built, with strong limbs and fearsome features, and addressed as 'nrihan', the slayer of men, he is constantly implored not to destroy or injure in his anger but to bestow blessings of well-being and happiness. He is entreated to spare the worshipper and his property but to destroy others with his fatal shafts. Fear of Rudra's terrifying wrath could well have been echoing current socio-historical conditions as, with the population rapidly expanding, people were settling in new territories and lived in constant dread of assaults from the numerous jungle tribes.

To Rudra bring these songs, whose bow
is firm and strong, the self-dependent
god, with swiftly flying shafts,
the wise conqueror whom none may
overcome, armed with sharp-pointed
weapons; may he hear our call.[1]

—Rig Veda, 7.46.1

May thy bright arrow, which, shot down
by thee from heaven, flieth upon the
earth, pass us by.
Thou, very gracious god, hast thousand
medicines; inflict no evil on our progeny.

—Rig Veda, 7.46.3

The theme of Rudra's sovereignty over disease runs through other hymns as well. He is described as a dispenser of remedies and, almost as a corollary to this, has dominion over healing herbs. We encounter this healing power in the early medieval period in the Puranas as well as in inscriptions, where Shiva is referred to by the epithet Vaidyanatha.

Where is that gracious hand of thine, O Rudra,
the hand that giveth health and bringeth comfort.

—Rig Veda, 2.33.7

O Rudra, praise thee, be gracious to the singer;
let thy hosts spare us and smite down another.
I bend to thee as thou approachest, Rudra,
Even as a boy before the sire who greets him.
I praise thee, bounteous giver, lord of heroes;
give medicines to us as thou art lauded.

—Rig Veda, 2.33.11–12

Do thou with strengthening balms incite our heroes;
I hear thee famed as the best of all physicians.

—Rig Veda, 2.33.4

Interestingly, the Pashupati form and a doctrine of the Pashupata sect, the 'pasha' or the noose of illusion, is referred to in the hymn quoted below.

Slay us not, nor abandon us, O Rudra;
Let not thy noose, when thou art angry, seize us.

—Rig Veda, 7.46.4

A number of hymns describe Rudra's activities and physical characteristics, which often coincide with what we know of Shiva. Rudra is a wanderer, he is strong, dreaded because of his wrathful nature. He has braided hair, his darts kill men and cattle, and he is a great physician. In one hymn Rudra is called

'Kapardin' as he wears his hair braided and knotted like a cowry shell. Even though in the Rig Veda other divinities like Soma and Pushan also have braided hair, Kapardin is an epithet used for Shiva in most texts of the later periods and Shiva's image is undeniably associated with matted, if not braided, hair.

To the strong Rudra bring we these our songs of praise,
to him the lord of heroes, with the braided hair.
That it be well with our cattle and our men,
that in this village all be healthy and well-fed.
Be gracious unto us, O Rudra, bring us joy:
Thee lord of heroes, thee with reverence we will serve.

—Rig Veda, 1.64.1–2

To Rudra, lord of sacrifice, of hymns and balmy medicines,
We pray for joy and health and strength.
He shines in splendour like the sun, refulgent as bright gold is he.
The good, the best among the gods
May he grant health to our steeds, well-being to our rams and ewe,
to men, to women and to kine.

—Rig Veda, 1.43.4–6

Chief of all born art thou in glory, Rudra,
mightiest of the mighty.
Transport us beyond trouble to well-being;
Repel thou from us all assaults of mischief.
Let us not anger thee with worship, Rudra,
ill-praise or mingled invocation.

—Rig Veda, 2.33.3–4

It has been said that the adoration expressed for Rudra in the earliest texts was neither genuine nor sincere, but 'utilitarian' as it was out of fear. Human worshippers would do anything to be on his good side and appeasement by flattery seemed an easy enough tactic. It is possible that the epithet 'shiva' was used as a pacifier to temper the ferocious nature of the god when appealing to his strength for protection and blessing. Rudra-Shiva is, then, a result of a kind of symbiosis arising from the response of human beings to certain fearsome qualities they perceived in their environment or in their own natures.

Though there is little concrete evidence to support the theory, some scholars believe that Shiva's origins go back to the pre-Vedic period. If Shiva's life story can be traced back to the evidence unearthed at the Indus civilization site at Mohenjo-Daro, he is the oldest 'living' god in the world. Unfortunately, the record of twelve centuries of that history is still hidden from view what with the script, if indeed it is considered a script (for even that is being contested), still to be comprehensively deciphered. However, it is important to keep these early representations in mind.

Excavations at the Indus sites of the third millennium BCE have brought to light what appear to be the earliest representations of Shiva. I am referring, in particular, to what has been called the 'proto-Pashupati' seal. Before we enter the domain of speculation over this seal, suffice it to say that it was first identified as 'Pashupati-Shiva' because it appears to depict an ithyphallic male (with a raised or erect penis) seated in a yogic asana, not unlike many images of Shiva found in ancient and medieval India.

The debate over what the seal represents continues to this day. The following interpretations will give an idea of the minutiae with which scholars grapple in order to arrive at a consensual agreement. The figure carved on the seal has three faces, with what appear to be horns, and is therefore often called the 'horned deity'. The 'deity' is seated on a low dais, cross-legged, more specifically in badhakonasana, a yogic posture. He is surrounded by animals, a rhinoceros, a buffalo, a tiger, an elephant and two goats and deer, which are under the dais. There is a seven-sign inscription on the upper side of the seal. To some scholars the 'horns' on the deity's head have appeared as flames; others see them variously as the crescent moon, a plant or a decorative headdress; and some have even wondered whether the horns are bovine and the figure is that of a buffalo or a bull, not of a human form at all. Others say that the face is fierce and has a 'tigerish' aspect to it and is not meant to be human or bovine. Some have doubted the gender of the figure, claiming that the 'erect phallus' is actually a belt, and have called it a female divinity. 'The mistress of animals', as they interpret it to be, is a goddess of beasts and vegetation. She has been identified as the archetypal mother goddess who controls biological regeneration and has a singular command over the existence and destruction of the biological world.

The many features that coincide with subsequent depictions of Shiva (the yogic posture, the ithyphallic state, the animals) have tempted scholars to label the figure as proto-Shiva. Besides, phallus-shaped stones and other figures in what seem to be yogic postures have been found in abundance at the Indus sites. The signs of an austere god associated with fertility may quite easily point to Shiva of a later period.

~

Shiva's history provides an outstanding example of the origin and evolution of a god developing out of primitive tribal life and linked inseparably with the social and material conditions of the time.

The Rig Veda 'shows' him with a bow (pinaka-dhrik) and arrows and later, with the use of iron, he is depicted with the battle-axe and then with the trident or trishul, a weapon necessary for hunting and gathering and also used by tribes of later periods, reminding us of the hunter phase in human evolution. In the Mahabharata he gives Arjuna the most powerful weapon in the guise of a tribal hunter. Later, the very same Shiva is no longer a lone hunter but is married and lives the life of a householder with a wife and two sons. He also excels in dance and music, among many other accomplishments. The modus operandi that enables gods like Shiva to encompass these myriad beliefs is embedded in a historical process of assimilation and in a human psychology that allows for such improvization. This process is not entirely unique to Shiva, because the same may be said about other Hindu deities who have encrustations of different regions, eras and media grafted on to them, rendering them at once syncretic and composite.

The brahmanical tradition has been continuously shaped by alternative traditions. After all, the brahmans were not composing myths in a vacuum, but were influenced equally by their own divine inspirations and the milieu in which they lived. In the Vedas, and later in the Puranas, one often chances upon a grudging admission to the lurking presence of the 'other'. Although references to the people who worship 'strange' gods and speak in garbled tongues are almost unfailingly censorious and harsh, they nevertheless give us some idea of those dwelling in the margins of brahmanical society.

Time and again the brahmans sought to establish their superiority in society either by dictating injunctions pertaining to different sets of people or through the creation of myths that were repeated again and again in subsequent texts, modifying the ritualistic world view of the Vedas. Nothing in Hinduism is expressed parsimoniously, especially the Puranic myths which are a veritable embarrassment of riches. In this commodious mass, the myths surrounding Shiva are in fact some of the most rivetting tales. Some are undoubtedly parables but many were created merely to entertain and to remind followers of the drama and richness of human relationships and behaviour. Only after ploughing through reams of discussions on mundane matters does one occasionally come across different thought processes. This is due to an amalgamation of ideas of different people, cults and deities which are sometimes inchoate and dispersed in nature.

In the Vedas, Rudra is portrayed as a merciless destroyer, and by the time the Mahabharata and the Puranas are composed Rudra-Shiva is associated with the destruction of the sacrificial ceremony, bringing peril not only upon individuals but to the very order of society as founded upon sacred laws enacted symbolically in the sacrificial ritual. In his contempt for ritual and religious rites, Shiva ignores, overturns and confutes the rules laid down by the brahman priests and they inveigh against him with undisguised hostility. Time and again one comes across myths that explain the anomalies Shiva is engaged in as he overthrows or subverts conventions and mores of the brahmanical world. In these sources Shiva comes across as a deity of other peoples who was gradually assimilated into the brahmanical fold, though his aberrant actions and strange nature continue to evoke alarm and censure.

Hinduism is a religion characterized by an ever-present dynamism where the divine is concerned. Within the large span of recorded history there seem to have been times when features found in one deity overlapped with those of others. As a matter of fact, some deities have actually atrophied and faded away from human memory and consciousness. Even though Hinduism gives the impression of being a rigid, orthodox tradition, in reality it encouraged inventiveness. Often, unpalatable features of a certain divinity or particular associations that could cause discomfort in the light of changing moralities were either veiled over or removed altogether. As a result, some deities have changed so much that their past is hardly visible in their present-day depictions. Vishnu, who held the same status as Shiva in the Rig Veda, is rarely depicted today except in the form of his avataras. Durga, who is today depicted somewhat coyly seated on her vahana, her legs to one side and clad fully and demurely in a sari, contrasts sharply with the way she is rendered in a remarkable sculpture at Mahabalipuram. There, Durga, in a short, skirt-like garment, is seated astride her vahana, with her legs exposed and a countenance which undoubtedly portrays a calm enjoyment of her victory. Portraying a woman enjoying a battle, even if she is a goddess and has just destroyed a demon, was evidently not acceptable to a patriarchal society!

Shiva's image, on the other hand, has largely escaped such 'sanitization' and one does not have to enter into an involved process of decoding his symbolization as there has been little bowdlerization. Even though one is loathe to reify the existence of a continuous, linear development in Shiva, one cannot sidestep the fact that many characteristics imbued in his earliest appearances continue, unfiltered and unbridled. This is clearly borne out in the imagery of animal-skin clothing and ash-smeared body, of sacred intoxication and frenzied worship by long-haired followers who are spoken of with awe and dread—accoutrements that render him fearful or antinomian. It must be said here that though certain practices and images may appear befuddling to a later sense of propriety, it is not enough to rationalize them as mere symbolism. One cannot ignore the fact that symbols derive from material foundations which had some practical significance at the time of their origin.

The religion of Shiva must be seen as an organic whole; Shiva's incidence in folk religion is complementary, not exclusive, to his worship in the brahmanical tradition. Shaivism is really an amalgamation of scattered folk cult traditions and

Vedic inspiration. Besides the folk element, Shaiva theology has developed as much from the prevalence of Rudra in Vedic literature as it has from the Advaita Vedanta of the Upanishads or the revelations in the Tantras and Agamas. The dividing line and the defining features are always tricky and any attempt to designate boundaries only draws one into murkier waters.

The osmosis that takes place between the folk traditions and 'high' religion leaves neither untouched. As the process takes its course, some elements stay local and others become pan-Indian. Regional forms such as Khandoba, a popular god in Maharashtra and believed to be an incarnation of Shiva, Mailara in Karnataka and Mallana in Andhra Pradesh existed parallel to the Shiva we read of in the Puranas. In the absence of a linear development proceeding in an orderly sequence from animism through polytheism to monotheism, the popular, elite, folk, oral and scriptural traditions all exist simultaneously in Hinduism. For instance, the 'aniconic' Shiva linga exists cheek by jowl with the most complex, abstruse, sophisticated Upanishadic philosophies. Fortunately, thanks to postcolonial studies, we no longer look at the Western, orderly way of perceiving subject matter as the best or the desired way. The idea that unilinear development is the correct progression of thought has given way to a happy acknowledgement of different, simultaneous ontologies. It is the accretion and tension of these varied strands that this book seeks to address.

~

Rudra-Shiva has been mentioned repeatedly in the Shvetashvatara Upanishad and in his role as Maheshwara he consolidates many of the diffused teachings of the Upanishads. In the realm of ideas we see that a crucial element of Shiva worship can be traced back to Upanishadic thought.

Shiva personifies the chaitanya atma, the alert one. For many he represents the pure, undifferentiated consciousness. Though he is unconscious of the material world around him (symbolized by his half-closed eyes), he constantly looks inwards and seeks for truth within himself. It is thus that he is in a state of perfect bliss. This aspect of Shiva has been encapsulated in the 'Nirvanashatakam', a popular Shaivite hymn, the refrain for which is 'Chidananda rupah Shivoham Shivo'ham', 'I am pure consciousness, bliss and the self; I am Shiva, Shiva alone am I'. This is 'ahamgrahopasana' and is based on the advaitic outlook of 'So'ham, Shivo'ham', 'He am I, Shiva am I'. The idea of being one with Shiva supersedes all other ways of worshipping him. Through grace, effort and determination, the devotee, the seeker of the ultimate truth, is led to a kind of communion with Shiva. Devotion to Shiva develops in the individual worshipper the consciousness of being one with him. There is an element of auto-suggestion that helps the aspirant in his path to 'sayuja', the ultimate identification of the individual with the supreme.

Such communion with the divine brings to devotees a heightened awareness of their own divine nature. In other words, in order to worship Shiva you have to become divine yourself. Within certain streams of Hinduism, it is understood that god resides within human beings, whereby men and women experience the capability, the dignity and the beauty of being divine themselves. This is the personalization of the phenomenon of mysticism, the interiorized experience of recognizing the ultimate reality. This aspect of Shiva worship is oriented towards the individual self rather than religious traditions.

The idea that drives the Shaiva devotee is echoed in one of the four mahavakyas of Hindu philosophy, 'tat tvam asi', which first occurs in the Chhandogya Upanishad, and refers to the divine consciousness of which the individual soul is a part. It also finds expression in the Upanishadic proclamation 'Aham Brahmasmi', 'I am Brahman', which is sometimes believed to be the boldest statement ever made by human beings in any age or part of the world.

The early Upanishads prescribe the practice of yoga in order to gain knowledge of the Self, that is, the atman, as well as immortality. Shiva is the great yogi who overcomes the opposition between immanence (vyavaharika) and transcendence (paramarthika). There are two aspects of Shiva's being. He is active in life as a householder and at the same time he is meditative. Immersed in contemplation he is the ideal of sattva, of poise, of calmness and of reflection. Yet he is also the root of all action. Shiva's dilemma reflects the classic tussle within Hinduism between dharma and moksha. Though they may appear as polar opposites, with dharma representing the temporal and moksha the eternal, Shiva seeks to reconcile the two. As in the dual concept of pravritti and nivritti, one belongs to the world and seeks to preserve it, while the other attempts to supersede the world and abdicate it. The tension between these two aspects of life and how Shiva reconciles them in his being is a theme that runs through almost all the myths associated with him.

The divine's ineffable nature is a standard leitmotif in some of the early Hindu narratives. It is firmly believed that the ultimate reality, that is, god, is unfathomable and beyond expression. The word often used for the actual experience of the divine is 'anirvachaniya', indescribable. The Katha Upanishad speaks eloquently of the failure of language to express the supreme: '. . . naiva vacha namanasa praptam sakyo na chakshusha', 'Not indeed by speech, nor by the mind, nor by sight, can it [the ultimate reality] be attained.' This gentle warning has, however, been regularly disregarded with some insouciance. Many mortals try to comprehend and expound, by different means at their disposal, the immortals they worship. This book is my attempt to communicate what I have understood of Shiva. It is for those who believe in him, as well as for those who do not necessarily have the same bhakti but are driven by another satisfying human emotion—curiosity, the desire to know how a god is created, how a god functions and, ultimately, how a god is cherished.

❧❦ Vishnu ❧❦

I am Vishnu. I nourish and sustain life. It is through my goodwill, sumati, that this world is perpetuated. Because this world is nourished and sustained by love, it is natural that as the sustainer of existence I should be seen as the embodiment of love; I am the god who ultimately inspires bhakti among worshippers.

It is a travesty to say that knowledge is the single and only correct path to god. No one can reach salvation through knowledge alone, without first dousing it in the rich potion of devotion. In the will to surrender completely, in the all-encompassing fervour of giving oneself, lies the power of the devotee. It is this power that renders bhakti superior to all forms of knowledge. My devotees surrender to me unquestioningly and wait patiently, wait with prapatti, a resigned devotion, for my blessings, for my prasada. As for me, if the devotion is sattvic, pure and complete, I am swift and give in readily, happily, for, after all, I am Vishnu.

I am Narayana, refuge of all men. I am the sanctuary, the ultimate resting place that mortal souls strive to attain. I pervade all directions, I penetrate all, I flow in and surround everything. I embody all that is in this universe, yet I transcend it. I am the numinous one. By my grace and magnanimity I recognized the potentialities of the universe and provided the one flicker needed to make it come alive and burst forth into this wondrous creation. It is through my essence, from the kernel of my being, that this world became animate.

I am Trivikrama. I astounded all by the three giant strides I took when I asked for an offering of three paces of land from the asura king Bali, who had come to be lord of the three worlds. How was he to know that a mere dwarf—for I had visited him in my Vamana avatara— could stride across the earth and the atmosphere in two steps and then, with the third, thrust him into the netherworld and claim the heavens? With these three strides I measured out the space where life can dwell. The first two steps were visible and marked out the tangible world. The third—the paramam padam— remains inscrutable to mortals, for it covers the glorious heavens which lie out of mankind's reach and beyond its conception.

I am Ananta, the infinite. Seated on coils of the many-hooded Adishesha in Vaikuntha, the highest heaven, I watch over the three worlds and reward the pious. I am the embodiment of the unspecified divine laws that preserve nature's equilibrium. I am the guardian of righteousness, the source of human morality and ethics, the lawful order of the universe and the foundation of all religion. Everything in the universe that gravitates towards a harmonious centre is me. I am the supreme protector. Whenever the world is out of sync, whenever right languishes or declines and wrong is on the ascendant, I return either as an ansha of myself or a purna avatara to guide humanity in a new direction—the right direction.

Brahma, Shiva and I—together we are the trimurti. We give form to the formless, nirguna Brahman, so mortals may focus their minds on the divine. Each of us plays our part in perpetuating the mystery of the cycle of creation and destruction. Brahma is the source of life, the creator; I am the power that sustains, nourishes and preserves life; and fulfilling the essential role of the annihilator is Shiva, who destroys the old to make room for the new.

Shiva and I are different in very many ways. He wears a wreath of human skulls, I am adorned with flower garlands. He is clad in tiger and elephant skins and serpents, I in costly garments and pearl strings. He is smeared in ashes and I in perfume. Where I am welcomed with open arms by one and all, Shiva arouses an inexplicable fear—not just in ordinary mortals but even among the greatest gods. His mere presence conjures up the gravest of portents

5

for those who experience it. For Shiva is wilful and impetuous, like a sudden storm that howls and roars and causes terrible destruction. His darts can bring dreaded diseases upon cattle and loved ones. And his passion causes mortals to engage intensely with existence—the dark side of existence. So wary are they of his terrifying nature that they turn into smooth-tongued flatterers when they find themselves face to face with him, beseeching him for mercy in their praise-songs, attributing all kinds of powers to him so that his anger may get diverted to someone else.

What neither gods nor mortals understand is that Shiva and I represent different dimensions of reality. Shiva, as his name suggests, is also the auspicious one, the primordial consciousness present in all existence. As the great lord of creation, the dancing Shiva, he personifies the energy and rhythm that bring forth life from the womb of the Brahman. His mysterious being not only comprises everything that exists but also epitomizes all that transcends existence. He is the great yogi who, through the grandeur of his inward search, guides the worshipper to unknown truths residing within. It is Shiva who provides the grace whereby the impurities that defile the self can be removed. So that when Shiva destroys he actually creates new phases of existence within a human being.

As for me, when I encounter Shiva and the stillness within him, I chant despite myself:

Pray, pray, for Shiva can harm you
Pray, pray, because you fear
Pray, pray, for he is a god
Pray, pray, for you know not how to please him
Pray, pray, for even if you did
He does not seem to care.

At the close of the previous kalpa, the three worlds—bhu, bhuvan and swarga—sank into complete darkness. As the worlds dissolved in a vast sheet of water in the course of the naimittik pralaya, as they do after every kalpa, the universe was left bereft of devas and sages. That was the first time I encountered Prajapati Brahma. It was a momentous event indeed, replete with the spectacle that accompanies such occasions.

I was resting on my serpent couch in the brimming ocean of milk, with Lakshmi sitting close by at my feet and surrounded by attendants, when Brahma appeared before me like an apparition. Smiling, he inquired, 'Who are you? How did you originate? What are you doing here? I am the progenitor of all beings: I am he who originated from himself! Get up and look at me, for I am your lord.'

A trifle taken aback at such bungling up of vital cosmic details, I proceeded to correct his gross misconception. (It is always preferable not to proclaim one's own glory, but at times it is imperative to do so to remove the veil of ignorance.) I said, as politely as I could in the face of such blatant egotism, 'On the contrary, it is I who am the creator

and destroyer of the universe. I have created and destroyed
it time and again.' My pronouncement hardly perturbed
Brahma. He said, 'I am the creator and dispenser of
destiny, I am the self-born deity. The universe is stationed
in me alone. I am Brahma with faces all around.' Not to
be outdone, I declared, 'The whole universe is situated
within me, O Brahma. Your way of thinking is like that
of a thief. You are born of the lotus that sprung from my
navel. You are my son. Your words are therefore pointless.'

Arguing with each other like this, each proclaiming
himself better than the other and claiming to be the lord
of all the worlds, we got ready to fight, like two foolish
goats out to kill each other. We met in the sky on our
respective vehicles, Brahma on his swan and me on
Garuda, while the devas who had gathered around in
little groups to witness the brawl moved about in their
chariots and scattered flowers from above, taking subtle
measures to keep themselves safe because they feared
for their lives. Infuriated at Brahma's brash arrogance,
I discharged blazing arrows at his chest, and he too cast
weapons of fiery fury at me. The battle assumed great
proportions as our attendants joined in the fray. Sword
clashed with armour, mace with trident, and terrible
weapons with ten thousand pointed spikes, flew in all
directions, roaring like violent gusts of wind.

Meanwhile, the devas who had been watching the
unending battle grew helpless and anxious. They discussed
the situation at great length among themselves and

concluded that it was time to call upon Shiva, the supreme Brahman, to restore peace. After all, Shiva is the source of all creation, sustenance, annihilation, concealment and blessing. Not even a blade of grass can be split without his permission. So the devas made their way to Kailash, where, bending their heads in reverence before Shiva, they shed tears of joy and presented their woes to him. Parameshwara told them he was aware of the fight that had broken out between Brahma and myself and was ready to proceed to the battlefield to take care of the matter. He then issued a directive to a hundred commanders of his attendants and set off, accompanied by his sons, Skanda and Ganesha, his ganas, the devas, and his wife, the goddess, amidst a din of musical instruments.

So it transpired that while Brahma and I were hurling weapons and abuses at each other—oblivious of the gods' endeavours to end our battle—a dazzling pillar of light was seen flaming on the northern side. We stared at it in surprise. By its splendour the waters sparkled, the clouds glittered; the entire universe was lit up by its brilliance. Intrigued, we hastened towards it to take a closer look. By now it was swiftly increasing in size and gradually it transformed into a massive column of flame piercing heaven and earth. It seemed stable, with no decline or decrease. It had neither a beginning, nor an end, nor any middle. It was incomparable, inexplicable and unsurpassed.

After gaping at it for a while, our heightening curiosity dulling our eagerness to fight, Brahma and I embarked on a mission to find the top and the bottom of the wondrous structure. It was decided that whoever completed the mission first was to be honoured as the greater between us. We assumed our well-known animal forms—Brahma the gander and I the boar—and I dived into the deep as Brahma winged into the heavens. We raced on and on in opposite directions. I descended further and further until I penetrated through the netherworld into unimaginable depths. On and on I plunged, but I failed to locate the root of the fiery column. Utterly exhausted, I returned to the battlefield just in time to see Brahma swooping in, looking rather triumphant. When I told him I had been unsuccessful in my mission, he danced with joy and proclaimed that he had sighted the tip of the column. 'Are you now ready to bow before me and acknowledge my superiority?' he asked.

At that instant, the side of the prodigious column burst open and, to our amazement, out stepped the lord of the linga, revealing himself in the niche-like aperture. That was how Shiva appeared before us—the supreme force, the very source of the universe. The eye on his forehead shone brightly and his matted locks embellished his broad shoulders. A garland of wonderful shape, wreathed with the sun, the moon, the planets and the stars hung to his feet, and in his hand he wielded a trident. I bent down to touch his feet, while Brahma stood beside me, visibly shaken, for he had tricked me into believing that he had reached the top of the pillar and knew that he would now have to face the consequences of his blatant, haughty falsehood. This was no ordinary pillar, whose beginning and end could be gauged! This was Shiva himself! As we bowed before him, Shiva thundered, 'I am Hara, the creator, preserver and destroyer of the three worlds and all that they hold. When the worlds meet their doom, all shall dissolve into me.'

'Forgive us, Lord,' I said. 'Our actions resulted from ignorance and delusion about you, whose body is without a beginning. You are the greatest, for neither your origin nor your end is known to anyone. O master of the worlds, you are the great Brahman, the supreme lord.' Turning to Brahma, who now looked quite deflated and contrite, I said, 'This eternal one created you, Brahma, and gave the Vedas unto you. Understand me to be only another form of him—the form that is eternal, the source of the origin of the universe.'

At these words, Shiva's voice softened, and he said, 'Hari, I am pleased because you remained true in spite of your desire to be supreme. Hence, among mortals you will have a following equal to mine. You will be honoured like me and, hereafter, will be worshipped in separate temples by devoted followers.' Then he turned to Brahma and, catching hold of a tuft of the hair on Brahma's fifth head, which was guilty of uttering the gross lie, he furiously shook his trident and chopped it off, saying, 'But you, Brahma, in order to extort honour from gods and mortals you assumed the role of the lord in a roguish manner. There shall be no temples built for you. No one shall worship you, no rituals will be performed to please you or appease you.' I looked at Brahma's pitiful condition and entreated Shiva, 'Forgive him, O Mahadeva, for you are Ashutosha, who is easily pleased. By means of possessing yogic power you are Parameshwara, the unchanging lord and master. Allow Brahma to seek refuge in you, O ruler of the universe.' Brahma too fell at Shiva's feet and beseeched him, expressing utmost regret at his hasty and unthinking actions. Quickly pacified, Shiva the all-forgiving granted Brahma pardon and Brahma's remaining heads were saved from within an inch of Shiva's mighty trishul.

Shiva's path and mine have crossed many times after this encounter. There was a time when the rishis of Daruvana, the thick pine forest in the Himalaya, came to believe that there was no use in worshipping Shiva, or following his doctrine of detachment from the world to achieve salvation. Choosing an alternative path in their quest for moksha, they proceeded to perform ritual sacrifices and practised austerities as prescribed in the Vedas and the Smarta texts and even commanded their wives and sons to engage only in the activities useful for the purpose of daily living. Observing them from his mountain residence, Shiva decided to intervene and teach the sages a new and superior form of religious practice: the worship of his linga.

Before he set out on this task, Mahadeva summoned me to Kailash and said, 'Beloved Hari, you must assume the form of Mohini and enter the abode of the rishis in Daruvana. These rishis have no regard for me now. They are treading the wrong path. Go, excite their passions and delude them. Destroy their vratas.' So I assumed the female form of the bewitchingly beautiful celestial courtesan Mohini and accompanied Shiva to the mountain forest. As Mohini I had a full-moon face and a gleaming smile. My dark doe-eyes sparkled against my translucent skin. My breasts were round and firm and my anklets jingled invitingly as I moved about, as graceful as a swan.

Shiva, meanwhile, had disguised himself as a mendicant. He wore ragged, dirty bits of clothing. His eyes were feverish, his body was covered with ash. He held a begging bowl in his hand and bared his teeth in a terrifying way. When he laughed, there emanated a terrible animal-like sound that could chill the bones of mortals. Together we walked, hand in hand, like brother and sister, till our paths diverged.

The moment I came within their sight, the rishis of Daruvana seemed to lose sense of their faculties and began to behave like they could no longer exercise their powers of understanding and discretion. They followed me around, their eyes burning with lust. While they were occupied with me, Shiva entered their dwellings and lured their wives into a web of desire. The rishis' wives followed him in slow, unfocussed gait, their hips swinging enticingly, heavy with desire. Some had their combs still entangled in their hair, their clothes half-tied. They entreated Shiva to satisfy them in a variety of ways. Shiva multiplied himself and appeared in the minds of the women. All of them enjoyed him heartily and in the morning brought forth 18,000 rishis with matted locks and holding dandas and kamandalus.

When the rishis, so long immersed in their own lust, found their wives improperly dressed, trooping after what appeared to be a filthy, uncouth beggar, they were at first rendered speechless. Were these wanton, reckless women really their obedient, morally attuned wives? As though awakening from a stupor, the rishis yelled out to them in acute desperation to behave themselves and return to their homes and children. But the women remained oblivious to everything around them except the attractive beggar who had introduced them to forbidden pleasures.

The rishis, who had so far not recognized Shiva, decided to hunt down the stranger who was causing such havoc. 'Kill him!' said one, 'Castrate him!' said another, as they rounded on him. Shiva vanished into the dense forest and the rishis split up into groups to search for him. In the forest, as Pashupati, the lord of beasts, he mocked them, fooling them with laughter, howls and roars. Eventually they found him sitting on a log in a clearing. As they surrounded him, he said, 'You want to castrate me, do you? I will do it myself.' Calmly grasping his red phallus and scrotum with one hand, he plucked them out and tossed them into the grass. The rishis were mortified by this bizarre, violent action and, still unaware of the beggar's real identity, they failed to worship the linga as they should have. The consequence of this additional slight was inconceivable bedlam. All living beings in the range of the three worlds disappeared, fire became devoid of lustre, the skies darkened, wind and water swirled and raged.

As realization dawned, the rishis prayed to Shiva and asked for forgiveness. He blessed them and directed them to do tapas in the forest. The rishis acted accordingly and things returned to normal as they constructed a replica of the linga and began to worship it.

I have also been a witness to one of the most poignant moments of Shiva's life. It was the day I was called upon to perform a duty I would not wish upon my worst enemy.

It so happened that Daksha, Shiva's father-in-law, was preparing to host a mighty yajna, to which I had been invited along with the entire host of gods. Rumour had it that Daksha had not invited Shiva, or even Sati, the daughter who had once been the apple of Daksha's eye. This was not surprising, for besides the fact that Shiva was customarily left out of ritual sacrifices, it was well known how much Daksha despised him for not following the brahmanical way of life prescribed in the Vedas—so much, in fact, that his feelings of scorn extended to his beloved daughter Sati, whom he had not met or invited home since her wedding.

I was quite certain that, detached as he always is from worldly matters, Shiva would not be perturbed by Daksha's neglect—but, surely, Sati would not be content to remain quietly in their mountain abode while festivities were being held in her father's home. She had tried earlier to soften her father's heart towards her husband, to no avail. Would she give up another chance to reconcile the two men?

But Sati could not have been prepared for the reception that awaited her. When I reached the sacrificial venue I realized that not only had Daksha failed to invite Shiva but, in an ugly display of sheer arrogance, he had also planned not to grant Shiva his due share of the sacrifice. Before I could react, I spotted Sati entering the sacred hall. Shiva was nowhere to be seen, but his faithful disciples Nandi and Bhringi lurked at the entrance, along with a retinue of ghosts and ghouls. I watched with growing anxiety as the full extent of Daksha's offence dawned on Sati and she attempted to reason with her father about his attitude to Shiva. But clearly Daksha's audacity had exceeded all limits, for he heaped insult upon insult on Shiva before all the invited guests. To our collective horror, unable to bear further castigation of her beloved spouse, seething with anger and resentment, Sati summoned her yogic fire and extinguished her life. I knew right then that utter chaos and damnation would befall the haughty Daksha, but even I had underestimated Mahadeva's passion.

Informed by his terror-stricken hordes, Shankara arrived on the scene only to find that his cherished wife had suffered a macabre end. Shiva's anger, born of inconsolable grief, knew no bounds. We watched, aghast, as he dug his hand into his coarse, matted locks, drew out a single strand of hair with his thumb and forefinger and let it float softly to the ground. From it emerged the terrifying form of Virabhadra, red-faced, many-armed and with the fire of wrath leaping out from every pore in his body. From those flames emerged hundreds like him, yelling, shrieking, cursing and hurling abuse. They danced strange distorted dances and sang evil songs of hatred, crying out for blood and vengeance. They had crude weapons which they used to desecrate the sacrificial fires. They attacked the assembled gods, tearing out hearts and limbs and drinking blood. Virabhadra led them in this mayhem until he spotted Daksha. Wielding his heavy axe, he chopped off the Prajapati's head and flung it into the altar.

His anger spent, the bereaved Shiva now turned to Sati's remains and lifted her corpse in his arms. At first there was a dreadful silence. Then a low, animal-like moan gradually emanated from his throat, like a siren mounting to a crescendo, and he began to scream in anguish. Everyone cupped their palms over their ears and scrambled about like mice, running pell-mell, into each other, bumping into the pillars of the hall, knocking about the already strewn brass utensils. Shiva slung Sati's corpse across his shoulder and commenced a grim dance of profuse sorrow. It was a sorrow so fierce that it shook the world. Rivers ran out of their course, the moon refused to leave the sky, the sun did not shine, the birds, the animals, every living thing stopped procreating. The entire cosmos was consumed by utter chaos, its every corner filled with misery and darkness. The rest of the gods, unable to deal with the might of Shiva at the best of times, now stood around, helpless witnesses to his heart-wrenching grief. The scene was apocalyptic, to say the least.

In order to quell Shiva's mourning and save the world from ruin, Sati's body would somehow have to be removed from his arms. It now fell upon me to carry out this dreadful task. I am, after all, the preserver and I have to do my duty no matter how unpleasant it may be. I picked up the sudarshan chakra, my serrated discus and, muttering a shloka under my breath, I took aim and started to slice Sati's body into little pieces. As distasteful and blasphemous as this was, there was really little else I could do. Her arms fell off, as did her breasts; her feet dissolved into ashes as they settled on the ground. Blinded by misery, Shiva did not even notice what was happening. But, finally, when Sati's vulva fell on Kamarupa, Shiva ceased dancing and slowly returned to his senses.

Order returned to the world once again as Shiva restored the gods to life and, when Prasuti, Daksha's wife, pleaded with him, he forgave Daksha too and replaced his head with that of a goat. Then he returned to his mountain abode and immersed himself in tapas, forgetting the world and trying not to let the memories of his beloved Sati enter his conscious mind.

Another incident for which I remain exceedingly grateful to Shiva, as I believe do all the gods, hearkens back to a remote and distant past. For a while we gods had been enjoying our supreme status in the universe, meditating and sharpening our senses and hearing our worshippers' prayers. But over a period of time an inexplicable sense of ennui overcame us all. Everything seemed lacklustre and there appeared to be little enchantment in a godly existence. We had always looked upon the asuras with hatred, but now even fighting with them held no thrill. The asuras, in the meantime, were winning battle after battle. What if the asuras took advantage of the situation and took over the three worlds? Frightened by such calamitous thoughts, the gods, sulking and grim-faced, gathered on Mount Meru, where the peak passes through the vault of the heavens to become the only part of the mortal world that belongs to the other. Seeing their weary faces, I told them that the only thing that could ameliorate this abysmal state of affairs was the celestial nectar of immortality, the elixir called soma or amrita.

The gods looked at me questioningly, perhaps wondering why I was directing them along an impossible path. Indeed, certain logistical details had to be taken care of before we embarked on the grand quest. The ocean was vast, replete with powerful waves that seethed and swirled and foamed. How was it to be churned? Following lengthy, complicated discussions among ourselves, an intricate and precise strategy was arrived at. It was decided that in order to procure the amrita from the ocean of milk, Mandaragiri, the great mountain, was to be used as the axle; Vasuki, the king of serpents, would act as the cord to be twisted around the mountain; and I in the form of the tortoise Akupara would support the weight of the mountain and hold it steady. This task, we all knew, could not be undertaken without the asuras. It would have to be done with their help. The situation was contrary to everything we had previously believed in, but we had little choice in the matter. Everything depended on gods getting the amrita, and we decided we would deal with the asuras once the amrita was safe in our custody.

So we allied ourselves with the asuras under the false promise that the nectar of immortality would be shared with them. We then proceeded to the seashore and sought the ocean's permission to churn it. For a thousand years the gods and demons pulled the mighty Vasuki back and forth, churning the potent ocean and waiting for it to yield the nectar. Sometimes, in their greed, the asuras pulled too ferociously and the mountain whirled so freely that trees fell off and flames burst forth. Over time the pace of activity slackened considerably as the gods and asuras, exhausted from the constant activity, began to give in.

But this would not do, so I whispered to Brahma, 'Tell them, if they continue to churn the water, the ocean will yield much more than just the nectar.'

So the churning continued. But instead of nectar, which was supposed to float up to the surface as butter floats up from milk, a dark, viscous mass suddenly rose from the depths of the ocean. It emanated the foulest fumes. It began to burn people into ashes. Asuras, devas, rishis, everyone began to flee in fright, shouting, 'Poison! Poison!' Despite all my efforts I was not able to destroy the poison, for even as I approached the water my body turned black. This was no ordinary dark liquid; it was halahala or kalakuta, the deadliest poison in the universe! There was just one way out of this catastrophe.

I ran to Kailash along with the devas and Brahma to see Lord Shiva. I bowed low and said to him, 'O Shiva, you are the supreme divine! You are the source, the first fruit of everything. Only you can drink the kalakuta, the first thing the world has offered us in our quest for amrita. Only he who can destroy the world can assimilate its poison. Only he who assimilates the poison of the world possesses the strength of compassion.' Answering our petition with a grave, 'My wish is to please you', Shiva descended to the ocean's shore. As he entered the turbulent waters, the black mass lapped at his feet. The devas and the asuras watched in amazement as Shiva plunged his left hand into the kalakuta and raised it to his mouth, his face set in the expression of someone savouring delectable refreshments. He swallowed it effortlessly. To prevent the poison from coursing through his body like a silent, secret river, the goddess Parvati held on to his neck as she foolishly felt it would harm him. Little did she know that Shiva was not going to let the poison leave his throat and harm the creatures who lived within him. We watched dumbfounded as Shiva's neck turned a deep blue from the effect of the poison, reminiscent almost of a peacock's neck, and proclaimed him Neelakantha, the blue-necked one. In centuries to come his disciples have related the reason in a beautiful verse: 'O thou master of all souls! In order to protect the living and non-living beings that are within and without thee, thou didst neither swallow nor vomit, but retained in thy throat that terrible flaming poison which scared away all the celestials. Is not this one supreme act of service enough to establish thy greatness?'

With the poison out of the way, the churning continued and our combined efforts were rewarded with many riches from the ocean floor. First came Kamadhenu the wish-fulfilling cow and Kalpataru, the tree that grants all desires, then came the moon, the apsaras, white steeds, the magical Kaustabha gem and Airavata the cosmic elephant, followed by the goddess Lakshmi and Dhanwantari, the physician. At long last a white vessel containing the precious nectar of immortality emerged.

Instantly, the treacherous asuras seized the vessel. But we were not about to lose the amrita to those villains. Once again, I assumed the form of the enchantress Mohini and approached them, for who could escape the wiles of one as beautiful as she? And, indeed, so bewitched were the asuras by my beauty and charms that they willingly handed the vessel to me. I quickly passed it on to the deities, who drank the nectar and rejoiced heartily.

Thus have Shiva and I been allies in many instances to ensure the continuity of the world so that people may live blessed lives. We are, after all, different aspects of the divine, appearing individually and sometimes as one to help mortals decipher the secrets of the universe.

Once, the gods who had never encountered Shiva asked me curiously, 'O master of the universe, Keshava, tell us: where does Shambhu reside?' Smiling, I said, 'Here is Shankara, residing in my body, united with me. Do you not see him?' When they insisted they could not, I showed them the linga lying on the lotus in my heart. They bathed it with milk, and worshipped it with bel leaves, lotuses and aromatic aguru, and chanted the one hundred and eight names of Shankara. Then they heard of Harihara, the form in which Shiva and I exist as one. 'O Vishnu, how is it that Hari and Shankara, born as they are of sattva and tamas, dwell as Harihara?' they asked. We appeared before them, then, Shiva and I, as Harihara. With our three eyes and earrings formed of snakes, our waist covered with deer skin and yellow robes, our hands bearing the discus and the trident, the saranga bow and the pinaka spear. 'Obeisance to thee, O all-pervasive, imperishable one,' they called out, and worshipped us as one.

Ekam sad vipra bahudha vadanti. To what is one, sages give many a name.

Shiva and Vishnu present different aspects of the godhead to the devotee. The difference is evident in the manner in which they are portrayed in myths, in iconography and in the values and religious attitudes their respective cults engender. The idiom of Vaishnavism is fundamentally orthodox and professedly Veda-based, just as that of Shaivism is unorthodox, almost heretical to the early Veda-based religion.

To justify their differences, Shiva and Vishnu, are said to represent different gunas, and are assigned separate cosmic roles. To staunch followers, each of them is capable of performing the tasks of the other. Their pairing in sculpture and their coming together in many myths demonstrate the desire for reconciliation among myth-makers.

Due to various social, political and historical reasons, the principal deities of the Hindu religious system get promoted to a position of supremacy within their own cults over a period of time, sometimes retaining what now appear to be 'primitive' characteristics contributing to the identity of the deity. In the case of Vishnu these elements are visible in the avatara system. Today, and for a long time now, Shiva within his own cult is assigned all the powers and functions of the supreme godhead, which at a notional level he shares with Brahma, Vishnu and even Shakti, the goddess. His basic nature is, however, largely understood to be destructive and his images usually reflect this in explicit symbolism, however peaceful or erotic the mood of the icon may be. In searching for Shiva's essential identity one has to go back to the Vedas, where it is clear that the archaic god of storm, disease and death—Rudra—constituted one of the most significant elements of the Shiva concept in Hinduism (see Introduction).

Symbolic Representation of the Deities: The Avataras and the Linga

Vishnu's avataras

While Shiva is symbolized by the single, featureless linga, Vishnu represents the idea of the multiplicity of forms.

This unique doctrine associated with Vishnu, and prevalent in the Puranas and epics, is called the avatara system. The word 'avatara' is composed of the verb root 'tri', which means to 'cross over', and the prefix 'ava', which connotes the descent of god from the eternal to the temporal realm. By this process a relatively minor Vedic god—in this case, Vishnu—becomes a major deity through a process of assimilating several other deities. (Deities are given 'minor' and 'major' status depending on the number of hymns solely dedicated to them in the Rig Veda, the earliest of the Vedic texts. By this count, in the Vedic pantheon, Indra, Agni and Vayu are major deities, while Vishnu—with just five hymns addressing him—and Rudra—with merely two and a half—are minor.) It is questionable whether the deities who became his avataras were initially subordinate to him, or even had anything to do with him, but by and by, through a theological sleight of hand, they became manifestations of him—transformations of his substance (vibhavas), or fragments of his being (anshas)—each of them upholding in some way the Vaishnava idiom.

Vishnu's pervasiveness and his readiness to help man in times of trouble are unmistakable traits of his character. The most important theological construct in the religion of Vishnu is his ability to incarnate himself on earth, in human, anthropomorphic or animal form, whenever dharma languishes. Even when the avataras employ what appear to be deceitful and therefore adharmic ways, it is always in the name of dharma, the principle which keeps the world habitable for man. For instance, in the Vishnu Purana we are told that Vishnu employed his power, yogamaya, to be born as Buddha in order to delude heretics into following non-Vedic creeds and thus bring about their destruction. Another avatara, Parashurama, exterminates the kshatriya caste a total of twenty-one times, when taking human lives is not the 'dharma' of a brahman under any circumstance. In popular perception Vishnu has ten incarnations though there are instances when he is said to have more or less in number. Two of his avataras, Rama and Krishna, the subjects of the two great epics the Ramayana and the Mahabharata, have undoubtedly aided his growth and popularity. The cult of Vishnu has among other features also been generally characterized by an atmosphere of love-play and sportiveness with explicit overtones of eroticism, to be found specifically in the worship of Krishna. To those who adore him, Vishnu is no less powerful than Shiva but he is always relatively mild and approachable, especially in the form of the avataras. This approachability is exemplified in the traditions of Ramlila and Krishnalila, among other artistic forms.

Emergence of the linga

The oldest, most fundamental symbol by which Shiva is recognized is the linga. Here, the definition of a symbol, without getting into the discursive connotations, is relevant. First, a symbol is an object or a sign that represents something else by association, resemblance or convention. Second, a symbol is the simplest depiction of a set of ideas and feelings. A symbol always has many meanings and may appear to have one or several at the same time. Natural phenomena, human or otherwise, turn into symbols when they assume meanings and roles other than those originally associated with them. Societies create a grammar of symbols to understand their specific ethos. Standards of ordinary logic cannot always be applied to these symbols as they may be culture and history specific. Parts of the body may also take on symbolic meaning, as the linga does in Shaiva theology.

It must be said here that the term 'linga' appeared in the Upanishads in its original context, that is, signifying a characteristic distinguishing mark. Later, the word went on to denote the specific sense of gender or sex. Brahman, the supreme divine, is described as 'alinga', that is, featureless, and subsequently in the early epics the word 'linga' was used to denote the most salient characteristics of an object or a person. Shiva's most characteristic emblem, the phallus, thus came to be called his linga.

Even though Shiva is also worshipped in the anthropomorphic form, the linga continues to be the most prominent visual aspect of his worship. Linga worship is the primary ritual act and the very essence of Shaiva theology. For thousands of years devotees, both male and female, have been offering worship to the linga, the main object of worship in Shaiva temples. The form of worship itself is uncomplicated. The simplest materials, such as water and milk, are poured on the linga; bel leaves, flowers, incense and freshly cooked rice cakes are also used in the worship.

Since it is not anthropomorphic but, rather, a symbolic form, the linga is often described as an 'aniconic' image of Shiva. Metaphysically, it tests the boundary between the seen and the unseen. The absolute Shiva, graciously choosing to enter the realm of embodiment, manifests and articulates himself in the visible form of the linga. Thus, it is often seen as the spiritualization of a physical form.

The linga is polyvalent, having many different meanings and forms, and, like all symbols, it means many different things to believers and scholars.

Shaivites consider it the central pillar of the universe, the unchanging axis round which the whole of creation moves. Its pillar-like shaft is seen as representing the axis mundi, the bridge between earth and heaven.

Some scholars have traced the linga's origin to the Vedic sacrificial post. The sacrificial post has been important since the time of the Rig Veda and there are several references to it in the Vedic hymns. Swami Vivekananda held that the worship of the linga originated from the famous hymn in the Atharva Veda in praise of the Yupa Stambha. The archaic concept of the 'yupa', the sacrificial stake of the Vedic religion, can be presumed to be the archetype of any non-phallic columnar construct serving a ritual purpose.

The linga also signifies advaita. Advaita is the featureless Brahman—non-dual, indivisible, unattached and without gunas, or qualities. In the Puranas we are told that Shiva alone is glorified as nishkala, nirguna, that is, featureless and formless, since he is identical with the supreme Brahman. But, at the same time, he is also shakala, as he has an embodied form. The linga, which gives form to the formless, manifests this paradox. For the devotee, the linga is the symbol of Shiva leading him or her to the path of advaita.

Lastly, the linga is considered a phallic symbol, and not just in an abstract sense. Joined with the yoni (vulva) of Shiva's consort, Shakti, it symbolizes the union of the male and the female principles—of purusha and prakriti, the passive and the dynamic forces that are the basis of the universe. The linga thus represents creation: biological, psychological and cosmic.

The phallic linga

That the linga in its fundamental symbolism is the phallus is often denied by Hindus today. Even an extremely well-informed Hindu is reluctant to acknowledge this aspect, thereby ignoring some truly overwhelming evidence in favour of phallic symbolism.

Early travellers to India were invariably shocked by lingas carved from stone. Very few of them remembered that the streets of Rome and Pompeii had been dotted with erect phalluses carved on stone plaques with inscriptions like *Hic habitata felicitas*: Here dwells happiness. Extending geographically from Athens of the sixth century BCE to the Roman Empire of the late fourth or early fifth century CE, there is evidence that the Romans worshipped stone phalluses as symbols of fertility with offerings of flowers, fruits and libations of honey, milk and wine. Priapus, the fertility god believed to be the son of Dionysus, is always depicted as ithyphallic. In iconography he appears as a somewhat grotesque figure with a grossly exaggerated and erect penis. Priapus was regarded both with amusement and affection, and was propitiated with gifts such as the first fruit of the land. He had a protective role, which developed naturally and logically from his fertility function.

The cult of linga worship is understood by some scholars to have been popular in the Indus cities as well. Small cone-like objects made of steatite and terracotta found in early Indus sites have been identified as phallic symbols by John Marshall and other archaeologists/historians on the basis of their suggestive appearance.

Early lingas were not just phallic symbols but were associated with vegetation, prosperity, abundance and fecundity. Round ring stones representing the female yoni and phallic stones found separately from the first century CE onwards indicate that the emblems of the male and female deities were worshipped separately. In later representations of the linga, the flat, projecting section called the peetha was seen to serve the purpose of draining off the water poured on the Shiva linga in the course of ritual worship in addition to being regarded as the representation of Shakti's yoni.

The merging of the Rigvedic Rudra with the phallic symbol seems to have occurred late in the pre-Christian era and was not recorded until the time of late epic literature. In the Rig Veda, Shiva is referred to as Rudra, but nowhere in the text is he associated with the phallus. The Rig Veda does mention a non-Vedic group of people, the Dasyu, who are described in the text as 'shishnadeva'. According to later commentators, 'shishna' means phallus. The exact meaning of 'shishnadeva' is unknown. It may mean 'having the phallus as their god'. It may also be referring to penis worshippers who employed phallus-shaped symbols like stones as their cult objects. In a hymn dedicated to Indra in verse 109 of Book X of the Rig Veda, the god is asked to keep the shishnadevas at bay and keep them away from a sacrifice. He is then described as having overcome them by attacking an indigenous stronghold with a hundred gates. The evil beings whom Indra defeats are called 'shishna rakshasa', 'spirits of darkness that vanish with the coming of the sun'.

In the Mahabharata ('Anushasana Parva', chapter 14), there is a clear reference to linga worship. Upamanyu, while recounting the glories of Shiva before Krishna, says, 'Mahadeva is the only god whose organ of generation (linga) is worshipped by men.' The sage further observes that as Brahma and Vishnu, along with the other gods, always worship the linga, Shiva is naturally the greatest among them. No being bears the mark of a lotus, a discus, or a thunderbolt on his or her body, he emphasizes, but all beings bear the male or female organ of generation (the linga or the yoni) on their bodies.

The Gudimallam linga in Andhra Pradesh (c. second/first century BCE) is the earliest independent icon of Hinduism. It is a fascinating piece of sculpture in that it establishes without doubt that the linga is the primary symbol from which Shiva originated in his recognizably human form. Along with the Aghapura linga and other mukhalingas found in Andhra Pradesh, it reinforces the idea that the linga is neither a mere symbol nor a simple pillar (sthanu), but is beyond doubt phallic in nature. The Gudimallam linga, whose shape is anatomically identical to the male generative organ, has a standing figure of Shiva carved into the front of the shaft and has no depiction of the yoni at its base. Shiva is carved in relief as though emerging from the linga, hence reflecting the lingodbhava episode in mythology, which incontrovertibly joins the two important aspects of Shiva as the aniconic linga and in the anthropomorphic form.

Here, Shiva is shown with full lips and thick curly hair (anticipating the matted locks seen in later iconography) and two arms carved in high relief. When a deity is depicted with two hands as against four or more, it symbolizes the deity's closeness to human beings. He stands astride the shoulders of a crouching dwarf-like figure, perhaps a yaksha or a gana, possibly showing Shiva's triumph over a creed where yakshas played an important role. Metaphorically, the yaksha or gana could be emblematic of avidya or ignorance, which is the noose (pasha) that constricts human thought and belief, about to be destroyed by the god who holds in his right hand a small horned animal (symbolic of sacrifice and death) and in his left a battle axe and water pot. The sculpture reveals many of the early perceptions of Shiva.

The worship of the Shiva linga gained popularity in the time of the Guptas, when linga worship became prevalent in temples all over India. Gradually the 'realistic' phallus got transmuted to a far more stylized representation that bore hardly any resemblance to the Gudimallam linga. At roughly the same time the Puranas began to preach that the linga represents the nirguna state of Shiva, like para-Brahman, and its worship is superior to all others.

The erect penis in the sense of the linga turns into a symbol when its meanings go beyond the directly biological—that is, the priapic state of arousal—especially since the roles it plays in myths and in the minds of worshippers serve goals other than passion and procreation. In the West, the linga is usually taken to signify a primitive fertility symbol and thereby acquires a sexual connotation. To Shiva's followers, it does not necessarily imply any erotic element and is worshipped as a symbol of the creative energies of the supreme deity. It has been the conventional image for so long that most of Shiva's devotees are oblivious to its sexual significance.

A particular school of thought takes the phallic interpretation of the linga one step further. To them the ithyphallic linga represents the unshed seed, the potential spiritual power built up by a yogi's religious austerities. According to this school of belief, the linga is raised in chastity, drawing up the seed instead of shedding it—that is, 'urddhvaretah'. The erect penis demonstrates the yoga of gnosis. The semen energy is transformed into a spiritual force that guides the worshipper towards union with the divine. The raised linga is the sign of the transcendental, the embodiment of creative tapas.

The linga in myth

There are two main episodes in the myths of the epic-Puranic tradition that introduce the linga. One is the lingodbhava or lingavirbhava episode where Vishnu and Brahma are also present, and the second is Shiva's encounter with the rishis in Daruvana.

The varying episodes related to the lingavirbhava or the

emergence of the linga are representative of the sectarian conflict between the linga as a cultic symbol and Vaishnavism or any other cult. This is because it points to the ultimate superiority of the linga cult and is an excellent example of the cloaking or disguising of cultic tension through the medium of mythology and legends in the Puranas, the epics and in folklore.

The lingavirbhava episode has been used in Bhakti verses to show the inadequacy of the bhakta or devotee analogous to Vishnu and Brahma in the myth.

O Supreme Lord! Thou ocean of mercy! Vishnu and Brahma, boring down, one to the earth and the other flying up to the sky as a boar and as a swan in order to find thy feet and head respectively, only got tired but did not discover the extremities of thy form. O Shambho! O lord of all! How is it that thou have become capable of being known to me? Pray does this conduct befit thee?[2]

O all-pervading one! Unto me, who am engaged in thy worship, vouchsafe eternal bliss at once. How could I possibly bear the grief, if as a result of thy worship, thou bestowest on me the position of Brahma or Vishnu, and still I fail to find thee in heaven or earth after searching for thee as a bird and a beast?[3]

In another verse, the devotee says that in this world there are many minor deities who bestow paltry rewards. The devotee does not, even in his dreams, attach any importance to them, to their worship, or to the results accruing from it. But he has prayed very long for a glimpse of Shiva's lotus feet, which is difficult to attain even for divinities like Vishnu and Brahma who live in close proximity to him. In yet another, the devotee discusses the ingredients of worship he has secured, but asks how he can perform the worship without acquiring the form of the bird or the boar, which went in search of Shiva's head and feet respectively but failed to get even a glimpse. Indeed, even Brahma and Vishnu who assumed these forms did not in truth know them.[4]

The symbolic appearance of Shiva as the manifestation of a column of fire is not surprising, as in early Vedic texts Shiva or Rudra is identified with Agni.[5] To those who claim that linga worship is not phallus worship but the Puranic transformation of Vedic fire worship, this is a substantiation of their theory. The Vayu Purana, Brahmanda Purana and Kurma Purana describe linga worship in similar terms. That linga worship is really fire worship is also exemplified in the twelve main lingas being called the 'jyotirlingas'.

In the lingavirbhava episode, Brahma falsely claimed that he had reached the apex of the linga, thus reducing it from a symbol of eternity to something finite. In his wrath Shiva assumed the terrifying form of Bhairava and cut off one of Brahma's heads. But there's more to the story. As the traditional deity of the brahmans, the multi-headed god cursed Shiva for the sin he had committed. For assaulting the archetype of the orthodox priesthood in his Bhairava form, Shiva was to carry the head with him as a perpetual burden and stigma until his crime was expiated. The severed head stuck fast to Shiva's hand and did not fall off until his guilt was expunged through penance. Other icons of Shiva carry a staff with a skull attached at the top (khatvanga) as a sign of his being excluded from orthodox Hindu society.

Shiva's visit to the pine forest introduces us to two key elements of Shaivism. First, the peculiar features of the Pashupata sect, and, second, to the worship of the linga.

In Daruvana, Shiva appeared before the rishis and their wives as Pashupati, 'the lord of animals'. He took the form of a nude mendicant wandering in search of alms, without caste, kin or acknowledged divine status. He is said to have approached his wife in this form as well, and begged for alms from her without being recognized. The Pashupata is the earliest known Shaiva sect. 'Pashu' may be understood as actual beasts, but in the metaphorical sense it signifies all human souls, fettered like sacrificial beasts into bondage. Uninitiated, ignorant and dumb, they must be motivated into enlightenment by god himself. All beasts are of Pashupati's flock, the wild and the tame.

According to the *Pashupatasutra* (Pashupata literature), members of the sect move through certain stages in their quest for salvation. These 'rites' are unabashedly and straightforwardly opposed to orthodoxy. In the first stage the Pashupatas bathe in and live among ashes from funeral pyres and perform acts of worship in the temple. In the second stage, the Pashupatas laugh, dance, convulse as if afflicted by a disease, make amorous gestures towards women, and sing, uttering an incantation, the 'huduk', which imitates a lowing animal. These antics are somewhat similar to the activities of shamans who have a deep connection with the spirit world. However, this is where the similarity ends, for there is an entire doctrine behind Pashupata 'rituals'. In general, such moronic behaviour and the use of nonsensical speech indicate nonconformity, but this stage is explained by the theory that the Pashupatas 'court dishonour' and thereby create an opportunity for their escape from the noose or pasha of avidya. The method seems to have been deliberately designed to attract attention through crazy antics and anti-social behaviour and shock the community into censuring them. The concomitant public disapproval would result in a fait accompli for the Pashupatas, who would acquire the merit of the observer who unnecessarily reviles them and transfer their own bad karma to their slanderers.

One of the five purificatory rites of the Pashupata doctrine is the removal of attachments. Through it, the Pashupatas declare their rejection of the world and isolation from it in true ascetic tradition, though it is an extreme expression. This kind of antinomian behaviour also ties in with the idea of the cathartic impulse behind 'acting out'. Through their abnormal behaviour, the Pashupatas give vent to repressed emotions, break individual social conditioning and free themselves from habits that characterize their everyday life and world view. In the final stage meditation comes to the fore, and in a higher stage of spiritual proficiency the Pashupatas abandon their sectarian marks and wander alone.

Shiva as Pashupati extracts devotion from the heretical brahmans by the alarming action of tearing out his phallus with his bare hands and arousing in them feelings of disgust and fear.

Other myths and what they reveal

The Puranas provide us with a rich and variegated mythology, creating a whole cosmos in which the 'bhakti' values of all forms of Hinduism are preserved, and flourish. The stories are told again and again as an institution of reminders and one has to agree that although present-day Hindus may refer to the Vedas as the foundation of their tradition, it is the Puranas which provide the myths and rituals by which their religious life is sustained.

In Hindu mythology, Shiva is so often regarded as the destroyer that his role as protector is seldom remembered. One of the episodes that seems very popular and finds repeated mention is the famous Puranic myth of the samudramanthan or the churning of the ocean. It illustrates two key ideas: why Shiva is the greatest among the gods, and the enormous value of the service he performs for the world by swallowing the terrible poison, halahal, for the well-being and sustenance of celestials and mortals alike. Shiva, we are told, did not fully swallow the kalakuta, as the halahal is also known, as he did not want to kill the creatures who lived inside his belly. Nor did he vomit it out as that would destroy all those residing on earth. Instead, he stored it in his throat and became Neelakantha, which is now a popular epithet for Shiva.

Bhakti verses recall his feat in the following words:

Did he not see even the gods fleeing from it? This wondrous act is past our understanding . . . What great compassion, what profound solicitude for the safety and security of his creatures![6]

In this myth, Shiva plays the role of the 'protector' who 'descends', so to say, to save the world. It is not just the mortal world that is in danger here, but a world where even the gods face certain destruction. Who better to tackle the deadly poison than Shiva who dwells in frightening places like cremation grounds and is surrounded by poisonous snakes and other antinomian elements at all times. Here, Vishnu, who is traditionally believed to be the preserver/protector, relinquishes his duty to Shiva.

The Shiva–Vishnu Combine

Mohini

Many important gods in the Vedic pantheon are attributed androgynous personalities. This is psychologically appealing, since all human beings have a male and female side to them and the balance of the two supposedly make for a 'happier' person. This may be considered paradoxical in Indian society, which is markedly patriarchal. But then, the world of the gods does not necessarily represent the world of mortals in every aspect. In the Vedas, Prajapati is described as an androgyne and has breasts.

The river goddess, Saraswati, is also seen as an androgyne. Her male spirit, Saraswat, is mentioned as early as in the Rig Veda (7.95.3) and also has breasts. Indra was known to be an androgyne and could stay among women in the form of a woman and among men in the form of a man, probably the initial concept of the Ardhanarishwara (see 'Parvati').

As for Vishnu, there are several myths in which he transforms himself into Mohini, the beautiful enchantress. At times this is to help the gods, even Shiva himself, and at times to deceive his opponents. During the samudramanthan, Vishnu appears as Mohini in order to trick the asuras into returning the amrita they had stolen away from the devas, while in the Daruvana episode he transforms into Mohini to seduce the rishis and help Shiva teach wayward devotees the right way to worship.

In fact, the Mohini account takes Vishnu's transformation to its logical conclusion. According to one version, Shiva is so enamoured at the sight of Mohini that he spills his seed which is collected by the seven seers on a leaf. They insert it in the ear of Anjani, the daughter of the sage Gautama, who in due course gives birth to Hanuman.[7] In a variant account, having heard from Narada that Vishnu was capable of taking the form of a woman, Shiva took Parvati along to meet him and requested him to show them his female form. Vishnu immediately transformed himself, but on seeing Mohini, Shiva got infatuated and ran after her. In trying to check him, Parvati clasped his phallus and Shiva released his semen on the ground. From it was born the god Mahabala.[8] The outcome of the union of Shiva and Mohini varies in different texts. Hanuman, Mahabala,

Skanda, and, more recently, Ayyappan are believed to have been born from it.[9]

The rational, materialistic explanation for the appearance of Mohini is that myth-makers transformed Vishnu into a woman to propagate the fusion of the Shiva and Vishnu cults and refute all claims of their hostility towards each other.

Harihara

Another form that brings forth the Vishnu–Shiva connection is that of Harihara.

A major force found in Hindu religious art and myths is the syncretization of heterogeneous deities. The paradigmatic image, more commonly known and seen, is that of the Ardhanarishwara, a combination of Shiva and Parvati—with Parvati, the dynamic prakriti, on the left and Shiva, the static purusha, on the right. It is seen philosophically as the interrelationship between the dynamic aspect of the divine manifesting itself as creation or matter. One way of understanding or explaining synthesis would be to consider the divine potential in deities as being interchangeable and capable of being transferred or shared. The two deities would then share dualized, collective responsibility and functions.

Although Vishnu and Shiva are opposites in the cosmological framework, a joint form, Harihara, is frequently mentioned in the various Puranas and in the epics, Hari being an epithet for Vishnu and Hara for Shiva.

There is, however, little specific mythology associated with

Harihara. For instance, in a dialogue between Markandeya and Brahma in the *Harivamsa*, Markandeya says that there is no difference between Shiva who exists in the form of Vishnu and Vishnu who exists in the form of Shiva. Together they are like the Ardhanarishwara. Any distinction between them is simply attributed to avidya, ignorance. The Vishnu Purana and the Vamana Purana also state that there is no difference between the two: 'Yo'ham sa tvam.'

The Harihara motif, which traces its origins to the early Kushan period (second century CE) evolved into a figure of considerable importance and presented definite iconographical parallels to the Ardhanarishwara. Structured on this model, it set two prominent deities of the brahmanical pantheon side by side in one reconciliatory image. In Harihara images, Vishnu, seen on the left side, replaces the function and role of Shakti. In an epigraph to an earlier book, I had delineated the distinct features of the two deities in the synthesized icon as: 'May the form, the form of Harihara or Vishnu and Shiva, grant you both enjoyment and salvation, which is both passionless and passionate, wearing both a wreath of human skulls and flower garlands, clad in tiger and elephant skins and in costly garments, adorned both with serpents and with pearl strings and other ornaments, and smeared with ashes and with perfume . . .'[10]

So far, historians of iconography have held that the real import of composite deities is that they demonstrate the inseparability or oneness of the male and the female in cosmic creation. While this is clearly a fundamental point, it does not address the implied hierarchical privilege that Shiva enjoys;

whether joined with Vishnu or with Parvati, Shiva typically represents the male and the dominant aspect of the pair.[11] The theological, philosophical and social implications of the male and female aspects of the Harihara image are rather complex and worthy of investigation.

Images such as that of Harihara offer instructive ways of thinking theologically about the interdependence of divine polarity in Indian tradition. The Harihara image reconciles the opposites of celebrating worldly life and renouncing its fettering enchantments.

By the time the syncretic image of Harihara appeared, the subordination of the left-hand side was already implicit in the composite image of the Ardhanarishwara, where Parvati is placed on the left. In brahmanical art, the left is subordinate in relation to the right. The Ardhanarishwara phenomenon thus indicates a subtle hint at hierarchy. This is sectarianism in gendered terms. The uneven balance of power between men and women in traditional patriarchal cultures provides the perfect metaphor for domination and subordination at the level of sculpture. Since Vishnu takes the place of Parvati, he is also placed on the left. It is possible that the image subtly denigrates Vishnu and proclaims Shiva's superiority. Yet, verses of subsequent periods render this 'togetherness' rather poignantly.

Lord Vishnu, who took many forms—as thy arrow, as thy mount, as thy consort occupying half thy body, as a boar, as thy friend, as thy drummer, and who offered his eyes at thy feet (in place of the lotus flower)—that Vishnu, forming a part of thy very being, most inspires worship . . . Who is there to excel him?[12]

As with Mohini, the union of Hari and Hara, is said to have produced the god Hariharaputra, identified in South Indian texts as Shasta (Aiyanar or Ayyappan).

Comparisons and Resolution

Broadly speaking, Vishnu's religion seems to be a cult based on a thoroughly patriarchal ideology, reflecting a settled varna-conscious community. Shiva's religion is more of an independent quest and, in that sense, an 'ascetic' creed, with rare display of pomp and grandeur. This may be quite confidently said about the tradition of Shiva worship and temples in North India.

Much can be gauged about the two male gods Vishnu and Shiva from the role their spouses play in their mythology and from their portrayal in iconography.

In the cult of Vishnu the goddess has an almost negligible place. Iconographically, she is entirely subsidiary, representing either the consort or an attribute, and has practically no independent status. Vaishnava icons depict the consorts Lakshmi or Bhudevi, and even Gadadevi in Vaikuntha images, as diminutive, subordinate creatures, almost in miniature, either issuing from between the feet of Vishnu who is the epitome of purusha, the male element, or as being blessed by the male god. Lakshmi is also depicted as massaging Vishnu's feet, a 'wifely' occupation in traditional Hindu society, as Vishnu himself sleeps on the serpent Ananta. It must be pointed out that such a depiction of Lakshmi is in relation to Vishnu alone, for Lakshmi, like Parvati, is an autonomous goddess. Her early Gajalakshmi forms, for instance, show her on her own, without Vishnu or any other male counterpart. She is also worshipped with much ceremony as the powerful goddess of wealth during the festival of Deepavali without being associated with Vishnu in any way.

By contrast, Shaiva beliefs are centred on the Shiva–Shakti dualism, of two equal partners represented by the sacred coitus, that is, the linga–yoni.[13] The oft repeated verse 'Shiva Shakti vihin shava', Shiva is a mere corpse without his consort Shakti, illustrates their complementary roles vis-à-vis each other. Shakti has a major role to play in the myths about Shiva. Shiva is an ascetic, detached from all things material, and is brought into contact with the external world—a crucial prerequisite for its smooth functioning—by Parvati.

In his relationship with his consort, Vishnu is paramount. Shiva on the other hand allows himself to even be trampled upon (sometimes literally, by the more violent aspects of Shakti) and the myths illustrate his frequent experiences of being browbeaten by Parvati. Ganga flows from Shiva's hair, while Vishnu brushes her with his foot. Lakshmi sits at Vishnu's feet tending to his every need; Parvati is of equal status to Shiva both in size and position, since she is seated either on his lap or on a common throne. Visually, the egalitarian status of the goddess to her spouse in Shaiva depictions is self-evident.

The reason for such a projection in perhaps that to an extent Shaivism evolved as a process of acculturation, absorbing tribal elements. Tribal societies accord an important place to women for their reproductive power as well as their significance as an economic resource. And they generally have a higher status in social, religious and ritual terms. These tribal elements are the impulse behind goddess worship; otherwise, in Vedic literature, we do not come across any powerful goddesses. Once again, Shiva fuses the Vedic and the non-Vedic; he seems to be the embodiment of the very shaktis that have been hitherto worshipped by non-Vedic people.

If we compare Vishnu with Shiva in this respect, Shiva may be said to have assimilated the goddess's shakti element more freely and with greater efficiency. The cults of Shiva and Shakti have combined to assimilate and absorb tantric elements in which tribal mother-goddesses retained their importance. Kali, a violent aspect of Shakti, is depicted standing on a supine Shiva, an aggressive stance to say the least. Beneath her, Shiva lies like a corpse, a shava. Kali is nude, but wears dreadful ornaments, specifically a garland of freshly severed heads and a girdle of hacked off arms dripping blood. This is the absolute opposite of the way Vishnu and Lakshmi are depicted. The asymmetry is not only one of different sizes but is expressed through the symbolism of the hierarchical relations between different parts of the body. In the Hindu scheme of body parts the feet hold the lowest rank. Thus Kali placing her feet on Shiva's chest carries a blatant message of dominance. Durga too is the destroyer of demons and a great protectress. No form of

Lakshmi would be described in such a manner or depicted in such attire as Kali. It is no wonder that Vaishnavism appealed to the royal houses, since strong male overtones are more conducive to emphasizing power and kshatriyahood. It must be noted, however, that Kali and Durga are just as fervently worshipped for their strength and invincibility in war.

Another reason why Vaishnavism is more closely identified with the brahmanical social system is Shiva's status as the pariah, the outsider (see 'Daksha'). Shiva moves around with bands of ganas whose social lineage is questionable. His 'polluting element' is starkly depicted in many myths and sculptures where he is shown carrying a bell, a practice that untouchables were compelled into: ringing the bell to announce their entrance into areas where the upper castes resided. By contrast, not one of Vishnu's human avataras is from a low-ranking caste. They belong, in fact, to families of kings and sages.

Ultimately, Vishnu brings a certain consistency to people's lives and a structure to society, just as Shiva provides elemental peace and autonomy to the individual, imparting the courage to move away from bonds, either actually through renunciation or mentally through detachment from everyday affairs. It boils down to the path one chooses while seeking spiritual succour in different phases of one's life. There is no doubt that through history there have been clashes between devotees of the two sects. The template of conflict and tension indicates that the two major theistic gods have interlacing mythological episodes that drive home a theological requirement, one of syncretism and mutual give and take.

~✠~ Sati ~✠~

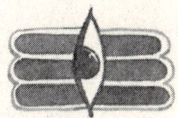

I am Sati, Shiva's wife, born for the salvation of the universe, the only one capable of absorbing Shiva's brilliance, his dazzling force. My skin to his, bone to bone, blood to blood, breath to breath—I was shaped for his desire. I alone can draw Shiva out of his contemplative stupor and instill in him the awareness that his participation in the universe is essential for its well-being.

My mother used to tell me that the day I was born, flowers rained down from the heavens as the gods rumbled their thunder drums and clear water streamed from the spotless firmament to refresh the earth, for I had arrived to be the companion of Shiva, the solitary one.

Kama, the god of love, had been unsuccessful to the extreme in his mission to get Shiva a bride. Miffed at having to experience mortifying extinction for his foolish efforts to distract Shiva from his tapas, Kama confessed to Brahma that his legendary skill at setting the most obstinate hearts aflutter, hitherto so rewarding, had had no impact on Shambhu. The delights of spring, the gamboling gazelles, the love-kindled prancing peacocks, the heavenly, delicate, embracing couples enjoying their tender dalliances and ecstatic joys—nothing could ignite the slightest spark in the resolute mahayogi, who persisted in his meditation, his senses under complete control, his eyes shut to the delights of the living world around him. 'I could not locate a single chink or crack through which to send my arrows home. There is no yearning in him for a mate, for a wife,' Kama had complained querulously.

Worried by the state of affairs, Brahma meditated on Mount Mandara for thirty-six thousand years, invoking my presence until I appeared before him. 'There is no woman but you capable of tempting Mahadeva's poised intellect, O Shakti,' he told me. 'Should he not take a wife, how is creation to continue in its course? He, the impassive one, is the cause of its beginning, middle and end.' It was up to me, then, to beguile Shiva and make him my own.

So I was born as the daughter of Daksha, patiently waiting for Shiva to realize that I was his 'Sat', his true, good, right and necessary consort.

I grew up quickly in the lap of love and luxury in my parents' home, surrounded by my sisters and being cared for by my mother. With my father I shared a special bond.

When he spoke to others in the household he did so with a gruff impatience, as though he was in a hurry to move away. However, he addressed me always with a tender attentiveness. Whenever he sought me out, I felt special, knowing well how rigid he was about his daily routine. He could not bear it if I were out of his sight for too long. Sometimes when I would be on my own in the garden for a while, I would hear my father calling out to me in the distance, his voice growing more anxious with every unanswered call. At times I would deliberately hide behind a tree just to hear alarm creeping into his voice. That was enough to make me happy, for my father was an expert at masking his emotions.

My father and I had so much to talk about that I think at times my mother felt left out, especially as he and I discussed matters of the mind. He instructed me on karma marga, yajna marga and jnana marga, and explained the main tenets of dharma, the significance of maintaining the sacred fire and the Sanskrit mantras chanted during a ritual sacrifice.

Once, he began a discussion on the importance of keeping oneself pure. This was a topic I felt strongly about, and I intervened, saying that, above all, our minds needed to be as clear as the fresh water that flows in a forest stream. Looking a little perturbed as he had not expected any interruption, he said, 'No. By purity I meant the observance of rules laid down in the Vedas.' He went on to tell me how imperative it was to memorize all the prayers to be chanted during rites and sacrifices and to know the correct procedure of giving dana and dakshina to the priests. 'Brahmans are the keepers of tradition, and tradition is everything,' he said. 'The priests are the sole repositories of knowledge and the intermediaries between the gods and the mortals.'

Usually I would just hear him out, but this time I interjected with my point of view. 'Certainly there is more to life than just the rituals,' I said. 'No matter how well executed, could rituals provide security to a troubled mind? Is it not far more important to look inwards, seek out perfection within ourselves and be in touch with our emotions? The world is after all an outcome of desire, and desire should be given its due importance, just as, at times, it should be controlled. But to say that desires are inconsequential as compared to the perfect execution of rituals—I'm afraid I do not agree with that.'

I could sense my father's displeasure at my words, but he did not voice them. Neither did I ever pursue such a discussion threadbare. What was the use? It would have left us eyeing each other uneasily and dented our feelings of love and mutual admiration. I was his favourite child and we guarded our relationship cautiously; somewhere in the back of our minds, perhaps, we realized its frailty.

All the talk of rites, rituals and scriptures and my father's obsession with such matters made me curious about his work. Sometimes I would crouch noiselessly behind walls or sit uncomfortably on my haunches for hours, watching him perform rites or discuss matters with other rishis. A couple of times my irritating sisters found me watching his activities intently. 'Why are you hiding here, Sati? What are you doing?' they hollered. My father looked up, startled at the disturbance and as our eyes locked, I fled from the hall to the inner chambers. What was so important in his work, I wondered, that kept him away from us for such long hours, and even at mealtimes? Tired of waiting for him, my mother would nod off to sleep, and when he finally made an appearance, exclaiming how hungry he was, she would not say a word though her eyes would take on a familiar resigned look. I was concerned about his fixation with rituals. He seemed to enjoy them, but to me they felt like afflictions that clung to him. Enjoyment should set one free, whereas there was always something in my father's eyes that led me to believe that an invisible burden weighed on his mind.

Nonetheless, I loved my father immensely. He was the only one in my family with whom I felt a special connection. My mother's love could not go beyond concern for my physical well-being, as she was perpetually scrambling hither and thither for my father's routine requirements, and although I loved my sisters, I found them to be quite tiresome at times. Somehow, I could never bring myself to be involved in their shrieking, giggling and nudging, or in their interest in lavish garments and intricate jewellery, or the hours they spent discussing their future husbands and arguing over whose would be more handsome and whose more intelligent. My mind was consumed by my desire to be with Shiva, to live a life of bliss by his side on the snow-clad peaks of the mighty Himalaya. I lived my life cocooned in this reverie.

Ah, Shiva! My mother once mentioned that his name was the first word I had lisped as an infant! Thoughts of his distant eyes and detached bearings had me perpetually entranced.

But my path to Shiva's side seemed filled with obstacles. When I told my parents I wanted Shiva as my husband, they could not believe their ears. My father, especially, balked at the very sound of his name. 'What did you say? Shiva!' he thundered. 'Do you know his lineage? Do you know where he lives? Does he have any comforts to provide you with? And when he leaves you alone and goes off with his ganas into the wilderness, what pray, my intelligent daughter, do you hope to do then?' Indeed, I had seen my father furious before, for he frequently lost his temper, but I had never been at the receiving end of his anger and impatience. His sarcastic comments stung my ears and I was dismayed to see the intensity of his revulsion to Shiva, which he now directed towards me.

I retaliated with a stubborn silence. I did not speak to either of my parents for days. I went about the motions of eating meals with the family and performing ritual worship of the gods without any communication with them. I remember quite well the indignant look in my father's eyes and the way my mother would try to involve me in a chat about some mundane issue just to break my silence. After all, we do not plan whom we are going to love; we can never say that a person possesses certain ideal characteristics and is therefore worthy of our love. We just love; it is as simple as that. Besides, while I could well understand how intimidating Shiva could be— his attire, his companions, and his remoteness that appeared to be hauteur were all completely alien to my father's way of life—it still rankled that my father never once considered my emotions. I was my father's favourite child; how could he not attempt to understand the feelings I cherished? Would my emotions, so enduring, so pure, be buried in the tussle between the two men? Such thoughts wrung my heart and I cried myself to sleep almost every night.

Opposed as my father was to giving my hand in marriage to Shiva, he had little choice. I was deeply in love with Shiva and, fortunately for me, my father could not ignore my grandfather Brahma's wish that we be united.

I clearly remember the day of our wedding. Shiva arrived, seated on his mount, Nandi, the magnificent bull. He was clad in the tiger-skin loincloth of the yogi, with a live serpent draped across his left shoulder and chest instead of the sacred brahmanical thread. Chandra, the moon, rested in his hair, suffusing him in a silvery light.

A serene smile played on his lips, spreading tranquility around him. His companions—some lesser, grotesque duplications of Shiva himself, some just misshapen beings—were jubilant and tumultuous. Blasting trumpets of shell and playing flutes of reed, they thumped kettledrums and tambourines, clapped their hands to the beat of time and careened through the air with piercing shrieks of joy. What a mighty din they made! The gods, though a little taken aback at first, soon joined in the festive parade. Fortunately, protocol took precedence over my father's disapproval of Shiva being my groom and his disappointment with me. Seeking to maintain his distance from Shiva and his hordes, he busied himself with receiving the distinguished guests, requesting them to be seated, offering water to wash their feet and arranging for their entertainment.

When it was time for us to leave, I sought out my parents to take their blessings. As my mother hugged me, I noticed a slow tear sliding down her cheek. My sisters followed, and they too seemed sad to see me go. But my father barely looked at me when I kneeled before him. For a moment my heart felt heavy at the thought that I did not know when I would see them again. But as I turned to face Shiva, all the negative thoughts in my mind vanished. Gently placing his hands on my waist, almost as though I would break if he gripped me too tightly, Shiva lifted me on to Nandi's back. The first time Shiva touched me, I thought my desire for him would burn me up from inside and I lowered my eyes so no one would see the raw craving in them. The entire assembly of gods, demons and earthly creatures, who had gathered to bid us farewell, raised an immense shout of exultation as we began our journey to my new home.

As the guests sped by on their magnificent chariots, Nandi ambled through dense forests and along mountain trails and stony pathways. I was content just to be with Shiva. At times he would embrace me with his strong hands to steady me and prevent me from falling, characteristically oblivious to the effect this had on me. I fell deeper and deeper into the abyss of his being, shameless in my want. Then Shiva asked me where I wanted to live. 'O beautiful maiden,' he said, 'tell me where you wish to stay: in Kailash which is pure and holy by virtue of the waters of Ganga, and lustrous like the full moon, or on the picturesque Mount Meru where the wives of sages recite and chant hymns in the caves and ridges, or in places full of deer and hundreds of lotus lakes? I shall make arrangements as you choose.' When I revealed my wish to live on the Himalayan peaks with him, Mahadeva smiled knowingly—the way only he can smile, the way only he can know.

As we approached Kailash, the magnificent mountain and its surroundings took my breath away. It appeared as though the scenery had leapt out of my fantasies just to make my new life seem blessed. Arising from amidst crystalline clouds, Kailash looked resplendent in grassy plains, shimmering lakes and thick forests. Multihued lotuses and blue lilies bloomed in abundance here and the boughs of trees laden with fruits and blossoms buzzed with the humming of bees. Flocks of swans, geese, cranes and peacocks swam and danced about as the cuckoo bird's sonorous call reverberated through the air. Ashvamukhas, apsaras and guhyakas roamed the greens as vidyadharis, kinnaris and other celestial damsels played on lutes, tabors and drums and danced in sensual delight. And there were the mountains themselves, mighty and majestic, their different moods reflecting the rising and setting of the sun, the darkness of moonless nights and the twinkling of the stars.

Alighting on the soft grass, I strolled around taking in the splendour of my surroundings, being greeted by those who had gathered to welcome me to my new home. Before long I heard Shiva dismissing everyone, including Nandi, who otherwise never left Shiva's side. 'Leave us alone,' he commanded, adding, 'but if I even think of you, immediately be at hand.' When they had left, I turned to Shiva with a question, even as he enfolded me in his arms: 'But where is our house, lord, will we have no roof over our heads?' Shiva smiled and replied, 'I am always without a house, for I wander in the wilderness, as an ascetic must. As for the roof, my love, the place we are in is the roof of the world, so what roof will there be above us?'

And so, in those magical surroundings, Shiva and I consummated our marriage as spring worked its magic around us. The trees and vines blossomed in unison and the lotus chalices on the lakes swayed gently as aromatic winds wafted by. Bees swarmed about, dizzied by fragrances fit to unsettle the senses of the steadiest of saints. When I gave myself to Shiva it was as though I were melting into his body, drowning in his fire. And when Shiva swallowed the nectar of my mouth as though he were sipping the divine liquor of immortality from the moon-cup, he seemed to be filled with unflagging desire and knew nothing of the exhaustion known to men.

In the secrecy of our solitude, among the bowers and caves, we knew only the ravishment of love. Shiva found place and pleasure only with me, and I with him. He would not be happy even for an instant without me. His eyes traced my every movement when I moved away from him to attend to some task. There were times when he followed me wherever I went. I would laugh self-consciously and ask him, 'Why are you following me?' In reply, he would give me a piercing look as if to tell me I should know the answer. Often he would disappear for short durations and return with heaps of lotus blossoms and wood flowers he had gathered for me, and proceed to decorate my hair and limbs with them. When I looked at myself in the mirror he would step up behind me and watch me admiring myself. He would release my night-dark hair from its clasp, let it fall around my face and then remove it gently from my forehead and eyes. He would beautify my feet with scarlet lac. He would whisper into my ear what he could just as well have spoken aloud, just so he could bring his face close to mine. He would set a spot of musk on my breast and draw closer to me saying he just wanted a whiff of the alluring fragrance. Sometimes he would lift the pearl necklaces adorning my neck and set them back in a different arrangement just to touch me. Whether he was fiddling with my jewellery or undoing the knots of my clothing, he always had the same look of concentration, his focus entirely on what he was doing, unmindful of the sensations he was arousing in me. In the frolic of our majestic love, Shiva would endeavour with boyish enthusiasm to surprise me with new ideas for us to entertain ourselves. By means of his art he would make himself invisible, then startle me with an embrace that made me dizzy with fright and longing.

When we reached satiety in our love-making, we would joke and laugh and have lengthy discussions. One day I said to him, 'O lord of lords, great yogi, you are beyond sattva, rajas and tamas, you are both saguna and nirguna, and free from aberration. I wish to know the principle whereby living beings surmount worldly miseries and obtain heaven.'

Shiva replied, 'Know, O beloved, that perfect knowledge or consciousness of my true nature leads to salvation. I am Brahman. A person who is engrossed in his devotion to me enjoys perpetual happiness. Devotion attracts me,

Sati, and my grace is bestowed on the lives of my true
devotees even if they be baseborn or outcast.'

When I presented him with more probing questions
about the ultimate means to salvation, he explained to
me that salvation is attained the moment a jiva removes
avidya and realizes that he or she is after all a part of
the universal spirit, the universal soul. 'All is one,'
said Shiva, cryptically. 'You are me, and I am that.' I
understood this, for did I not feel as though my soul
had expanded to accommodate the entire universe when
I was doing tapas?

As time went by and we settled into comfortable
domesticity, I found Shiva often unapproachable and
completely immersed in meditation. I understood his
self-absorption, I luxuriated in it, for I was aware that I
alone could draw him away from his intense reflections.
At such times, I would leave him to his contemplation
and walk by myself in the woods and glades. Invariably,
when I spent time on my own, my mind would wander
to my parents and my home, which I missed very much.
I tried very hard to reason why my father had been so
cruel to Shiva and me and looked for forgiveness in
my heart, but I found none. I thought of going back to
visit them and I knew Shiva would not stop me if I really
wished to. But my father's cruel words still haunted me.
I recalled how he always praised my sisters' husbands
and insisted that Shiva had dishonoured him and
possessed no praiseworthy qualities to speak of. I knew

my father was reputed to be wise but, oddly, he only saw Shiva's obvious strangeness and could not fathom the purnatva that was Shiva. I could not help wondering how long this impasse would last. How long would I have to wait to return home and see my parents and sisters again?

One day, hearing Shiva's ganas babbling excitedly, I emerged from our cave to see gods and seers, gandharvas and yakshas, apsaras and goddesses flying across the sky in their magnificent chariots. They were dressed in rich garments and gold ornaments and it looked like they were headed towards some grand celebration. Eager to find out more, I asked one of the ganas what all the excitement was about. He informed me that Daksha, my father, had been granted the prestigious title of 'Prajapati' by Brahma, and had arranged for a spectacular sacrifice and lavish feast to celebrate.

For a while I stood there in wonder, watching them flying by, enjoying the jubilation and festivities, feeling a sense of pride at my father's achievement. I could see him before my eyes, as he would look on the day of the ceremony, with his narrow, hollow-cheeked face and furrows on his forehead, eyes clouded in concentration, determined to perform the rites to utmost perfection. It dawned on me suddenly that I had not received an invitation for the ceremony. In fact there had been no word from home at all since I had reached Kailash. I felt tears pricking my eyes: Did my father not want to share this wonderful occasion with my husband and me? My sisters would certainly be there in all their finery, and wasn't I his favourite child? Perhaps it had slipped his mind to send us an invitation, I reasoned; after all he must be so busy with the preparations. I, as his daughter, should not stand on formality. So I banished all the dejection from my mind and, not wanting to waste any valuable time, quickly approached Shiva and told him of my desire to join the festivities.

'All the gods are going, let us go too,' I said. 'My sisters will be there with their husbands. I too wish to receive the presents which will be offered by my parents with you by my side. Besides, I feel homesick. Let me go and chat with my sisters and my mother for a while. The only company I have here is Nandi and the snakes that coil around your arms and neck.'

Shiva replied with an indulgent smile, 'How can you go? We have not been invited.' But when I insisted, he became grave and said, 'It appears your father's old grudge against me has led him to neglect you too. Although going to one's father's place needs no special invitation, arriving uninvited to a formal occasion is hardly the proper thing to do. Sati, my loved one, only those people go uninvited to such grand occasions whose vision is not prejudiced by their ego or their wrath. Are you sure you will not feel slighted? What if you do not receive proper attention or respect from your father because of his hatred towards me? I fear for you, my love. You are too precious and vulnerable.'

Hearing his words, and knowing in my heart that they were true, I no longer knew what I wanted to do. At times my fierce loyalty towards Shiva kept me stolid in my resolve not to attend the ceremony, to cultivate indifference and nonchalance like he would in such a situation. But the yearning to see my friends and relatives again, to be a part of a celebration I had every right to be a part of, overwhelmed me. I was miserable. I frequently burst into tears and wept in utter despondence, till my misery turned to rage which I heaped on Shiva. In those days I picked on him relentlessly. Nothing he did seemed right.

Things came to a head when one day Shiva reached the end of his patience and lost his temper. 'I am your husband and I mean to be obeyed. I forbid you to go,' he shouted. Already irritated, I yelled, 'Forbid? Did you say forbid? To me, who is the mother of all creation?' Without waiting any further, I set off alone, sullen and defiant. I felt no joy, no happy anticipation at meeting my sisters and my mother after so long. Instead, a sense of impending doom clouded my mind. I wept wretchedly on what seemed like a tortuous, endless journey, along the same route by which I had arrived at Kailash. Everything appeared different now, the enchanting beauty of the surroundings seemed to mock me. Suddenly, hearing a bustling sound behind me, I turned around to find thousands of Shiva's ganas, led by Nandi, following in my footsteps. Shiva had sent them to escort me on my way. For my entertainment they had brought along sarikas, the singing birds, balls, mirrors and lotuses, and musical instruments like kettledrums, conches and flutes. I was overwhelmed by Shiva's love for me. Yet my gloom did not subside, for now I could not help but imagine how ideal it would have been if my father had invited us with due decorum. And it unsettled me that I had left Shiva in anger, without even saying goodbye.

As I approached my parents' home, now bustling with activity, I found myself trembling, my nerves frayed by the thought of my father's reaction to my presence here. Not wanting to beckon ill luck with negative thoughts, I forced an image into my mind: upon seeing me, my father rushes forward to greet me, glowing with love and happiness. Almost a bit too obviously—loud, so everybody present can hear—he declares his regret at his invitation not reaching us. I eagerly lap up the excuse, however incredulous, and am placated for the moment. Later, when the guests leave and only the family is present, I confront him with my complaints and the sorrow he has caused me.

By this time I was at the entrance to the main hall, the sacred venue. I walked in slowly as the oblations were being made, subsumed by the rich smell of ghee, the fragrance of incense and camphor, the chanting of the mantras. All around me were sights, scenes, smells that were all too familiar. The sages in attendance, the vessels made of clay, wood, iron and gold placed neatly along the sides, the piles of durba grass, I had lived this scene so many times before. Looking around for familiar faces, my eyes fell on the place reserved for offerings made to the gods. All of them, major and minor, had been given their due but no offerings had been made to Shiva. A sudden rush of rage blinded me. Everything before me became blurred as tears streamed down my face. I could tolerate being slighted, even forgive my father for it, but this was by far the most audacious slight and I would not stand for it.

My mother and sisters approached to welcome me back home, their throats choking with affection and tears streaming down their lavishly decorated faces. My aunts offered me a seat of honour but I refused to accept it. With blood raging in my head, I barely heard my sisters' affectionate inquiries after my health. Somehow, the one question they kept repeating was, 'Have you come alone?', as if they were worried that Shiva had followed me to cause some kind of disruption. 'Yes, I have come alone,' I answered, my voice sounding strange to my own ears. I did not take my eyes off my father, hoping for some look of regret for having insulted us in this appalling way—if nothing, hoping to will it with my penetrating stare. But there was none. Instead, his face glowed with pride at the success of his arrangements and he continued to perform rituals oblivious of my presence.

Trying to keep my anger in check, and still hoping my father could provide an explanation for his actions, I approached him and addressed him directly. 'O Daksha, dear father, Indra, the king of gods has come here with his wife Sachi. Nirrti, the lord of the rakshasas, has come too. Vayu, the giver of life, has come to this sacrifice accompanied by fourteen attendants. Bhaskara with twelve souls, lord of the planets, and the moon, born in the family of Atri, have arrived. The eight Vasus, the two Ashvins, the gandharvas and the celestial nymphs, the vidyadharas, ghosts, vampires, yakshas and demons, goblins of horrible deeds and others who snatch life away, great rivers, streams, oceans, islands with mountains and wild beasts, the movable as well as the immovable—they are all here. Brahma's entire creation has been invited, to be honoured by you with gifts and attendants. But my revered husband alone is not a part of this magnificent affair. All this appears to me to be a void without him. In all probability you have forgotten to . . .'

My father rose to his feet and said, 'My dear child, hear precisely why he has not been invited. He holds a pot of skull, he wears a tiger's hide and has a garment of elephant's skin. His body is covered with ash, he carries a trident, and a garland of heads adorns his neck. He is naked and the cremation ground is his favourite haunt. He rubs his body with ashes. A snake is tied around his waist and he has put a ring around his organ of generation. He has made Vasuki his sacred thread. He always moves in this form on the earth. His attendants . . .'

I could not let him continue and exclaimed, 'I cannot believe you can behave inimically towards the lord who is above enmity. He is the source of the universe. He is the beloved soul of all embodied beings in this world. Nobody is dear or hateful to him, nobody is superior. It is your jealousy that causes you to maliciously condemn the greatest of the gods. You are unrighteous and look upon your inert material body as your soul. Hence it befits you to revile good souls. Alas, your honour has been sullied by your hatred for Shiva, who is the friend and protector of the universe. Great sages who long to taste the wine-like honey of Brahmanda bow at his lotus feet. You say that Shiva, who dwells in the cremation ground in the company of goblins, and who decorates himself with the garlands of skulls and ash from funeral pyres, is inauspicious. If it be so, why do the gods wear flowers fallen from his feet? Why do they run to him for succour and blessings when trouble approaches? When the supreme lord is blasphemed by unrestrained people such as you there are three ways to react to it. Either one should shut one's ears and leave, or kill the slanderer, cut off the vituperative tongue which utters such evil words, or lay down one's life. Such is the course of dharma. I choose to rid myself of this body, born of you, Shiva's slanderer. For the wise people say that the remedy for eating impure food out of ignorance is to vomit it out.

'It seems to me, dear father, that despite all your

years of collecting wisdom and knowledge, you have not understood a basic and crucial truth. Do you not know that karma is of two kinds? The first is what you and so many other rishis have dedicated their entire lives to—pravritti, in accordance to which sacrificial acts are alone important for the attainment of salvation. Nivritti is the other path which entails self-control and renunciation of this world and all worldly activity. This is the path of Shiva. You also need not entertain the pride that you are affluent and Rudra is a pauper, for the mystic powers, the siddhis, possessed by him can never be yours. Such powers are not attained in sacrificial halls by the performance of sacrifices. They are unmanifest, dependent upon our wills, enjoyed by avadhutas who have renounced all, while your path is extolled by creatures following the path of the smoke, who are gratified with the offerings at sacrifices. Yet you believe your rites are of supreme importance in this world, so much so, that you have excluded the symbol of wholeness from your invitation list. You offer sacrifices to all but not to sacrifice itself. The flowers of your rituals are rain falling from Shiva's feet. You see the unimportant things about him, his outward appearance and his raggedness. What about his wisdom? You say he has no home; do you not see that his home is everywhere precisely because it is nowhere? You say he has no family. Do you not realize that because Shiva is alone all the world is his family? He wears skulls around his neck and he is dressed simply in the four directions because he is detached from the world, because his state of consciousness is one of shunyata, of nivritti, of cessation.

'I have had enough of this impure body born of you, who have sinned against Shiva. Fie upon the birth from a man who vilifies a great soul!'

My mind was swirling with fury and regret. I thought of turning around and going back to Shiva's loving presence. But how could I return to Shiva after my father had insulted him? Shiva was not so petty as to mock me, but certainly he would think in his mind . . . And what about his followers in Kailash? How could I show my face there now? Better then to call upon my own powers to rid myself of this miserable life.

Amid frantic whisperings around me, I sat on the ground, facing north. I sipped water as achamana and, closing my eyes, I entered a yogic trance, silencing my mind before casting off my material body. Steady in my posture, I controlled paraana and apaana equally at the navel. Forcing up the vital air, udaana, from the mystical plexus, I gradually brought it up to my heart, holding it steady there. Then I lifted it to my throat and to the ajna-chakra between the eyebrows. My body was soon ablaze with fire produced by my samadhi.

In my final moments of consciousness the image I hold precious to my soul floated before my eyes. Did Shiva look just a bit shy as he stood at my father's doorstep on the day we were wed? And what was that in his smile as he lifted me onto Nandi for the first time? This much I know, O Rudra! I will be yours again. Since in this lifetime our love was stymied, I will be back as your beloved and we will be together for all of eternity.

The myth goes that Sati had closed the nine portals of her senses as she performed tapas, stopped her respiration and braced all of her powers. Her life breath ripped through the coronal suture of her skull and out of the tenth portal (the so-called Brahma fissure) and shot out of her head as her inanimate body slumped to the ground. The gods let out a universal shout of woe—'Sati shayati!'—and wept in agony.

Meanwhile Shiva, alerted by Narada about the tragic turn of events at Daksha's yajna, arrived on the scene. After creating Virabhadra and directing the terrible creature to lead the ganas in the utter destruction of Daksha's sacrifice, Shiva went in search of the body of his beloved wife. Seeing her remains lying unattended next to the sacred fire that, according to some versions of the myth, had refused to touch her, he stooped reverentially, lifted the corpse, placed it across his shoulders and walked out of the hall. Blind with agony, babbling to himself like a madman, he wandered the three worlds in frenzied despair. Seven times he went around the world with his burden, majestic in his wrath. The depth of his grief terrified the universe. The earth trembled in fear, the soil lost its moisture, the plants died and famine overcame the land. Brahma and the other gods observed this and were extremely troubled. They realized that Sati's corpse would not decay as long as it was in contact with Shiva. They approached Vishnu for help. With the help of his bow and arrow (some versions mention the sudarshan chakra, Vishnu's discus) Vishnu dismembered Sati's body and let the pieces fall to earth. The spots where the pieces fell are considered sites of magical potency for the worship of the goddess and are called Shaktipeethas. For example, the temple of Jwalamukhi-devi in Himachal Pradesh marks the spot where Sati's tongue is believed to have fallen, and Kamarupa in Assam, where Sati's yoni is said to have landed, is the site of the Kamakhya temple. Here, the vulva of the goddess is represented by two sloping faces of stone moistened by water from a perennial spring.

The Bhakta's Reward

One of the reasons why Shiva is so loved by his devotees is that his myths poignantly illustrate his many foibles which, paradoxically, emphasize his greatness. This is certainly not exclusive to Shiva, for one finds beautiful myths about the lives of other deities such as Rama and Krishna that evoke deep emotions, but stories such as the one about Sati are unmatched in their pathos and humanity. Where deities are concerned, perfection evokes admiration, but imperfections inspire love and devotion of a different order. Shiva is a mighty, unassailable god. His status as the immortal creator-preserver-destroyer all in one and his ability to control his passions are awe-inspiring, but the 'weaknesses' he exhibits are so essentially human that they induce true affection and bhakti among his devotees. Shiva's bhaktas do not have to strive to live up to ideals of perfection that their god exemplifies; inner calm and unwavering faith in Shiva brings them closer to the godhead than outward manifestations of perfection and worship.

Such blatant anthropomorphism in a god of Shiva's stature may be considered absurd, but it is equally comforting. Shiva's heart-wrenching loss at the death of his beloved wife, arouses empathy and draws the bhakta into the god's world. He/she wonders, perhaps, if Shiva should have allowed Sati to go alone to the ceremony. Perhaps, for once, he should have abandoned his 'detached' state and made peace with Daksha for Sati's sake. To the devotee Shiva's condition is all the more unfortunate when seen against the background of his way of life before he married Sati. He was a powerful, self-sufficient god, immersed in meditation, reluctant to embark on the householder's journey. Yet, when he eventually did partake of connubial bliss, he was left bereft and heartbroken. Ultimately, it is the familiar path, the stupor of detachment, that comes to his rescue when he is torn asunder by his grief.

Sati as Shakti, Sati as Woman

According to legend, Shiva eventually finds peace when he rediscovers his consort in the form of a yoni. He descends to earth as the linga, to enter into her, thus ensuring that they remain united forever. Thereon, Shiva and the great mother goddess in the Hindu tradition are inseparable. According to the Tantras (this part of the legend is not found in the Puranas), Sati's limbs fell in fifty-one places, which are called Shaktipeethas, literally, the seat of the goddess. At the peethas the goddess is the chief object of worship. The temples are erected to the different forms of the devi, not to the phallic emblem, which, if present, is there as an accessory not as a principal.

Shiva's relationship with the goddess continues to be a dialectical and taut one as in every lifetime she shares with him in each of her different forms—Parvati, Kali, Uma, Gauri, and so on—she persists in drawing him out of his preferred seclusion and involving him in worldly affairs. Sati is Shiva's first wife and in keeping with the Hindu notion of rebirth she returns as Parvati, daughter of Himavat and his wife Mena, to be his consort the second time round. It must be said here that although the mythologies of Sati and Parvati (as of the other forms of Shakti) are similar in many ways, and have probably influenced each other, each goddess's life is distinct enough to be treated separately (see 'Parvati'). The Shiva–Shakti myths emphasize the tension between asceticism and love and the reconciliation of the two. In the Sati myths, Shiva's involvement in the world is clearly suggested in the destruction and reinstitution of Daksha's sacrifice (see 'Vishnu', 'Daksha') and his descent to earth in the form of the linga to dwell with Sati's yoni.

Sati has a confrontation with Shiva over her right to attend the celebration at her parents' home. He forbids her to attend the sacrifice for which her father has made grand arrangements, but she forces him to let her go. In some versions of the myth, she leaves Kailash without his consent. Kalidasa's plays (fifth to sixth century CE) and the Puranas (c. 350 CE through the thirteenth century CE) narrate the central Sati myths in detail. We hear how Sati left for her parents' house with heavy sighs, her heart tormented by grief and anger, abandoning Shiva who is not only beloved of the saints but who, out of love, has given half his body to her in the Ardhanarishwara form (see 'Parvati'). The Bhagavat Purana describes how thousands of Shiva's followers, including his personal attendants and yakshis, led by Nandi, followed her with hearts saddened by her disobedience of Shiva. In fact the Bhagavat Purana explicitly states that Sati lost her sense of judgement due to her 'womanly' behaviour! Not a very welcome statement about a great goddess whom men and women look up to and whom women may want to emulate. This was probably to cover the embarrassment caused by very natural human behaviour, though not behoving a goddess of a patriarchal society. Not surprisingly, when Shiva reacts like a particularly vulnerable 'man', weeping inconsolably at the loss of his wife, his behaviour is not characterized as 'ungodly' or human.

In a sense, the Sati myth illustrates the goddess's strength and her superiority to Shiva. This idea receives further elaboration in Tantric scriptural and visual material where she is shown as the superior power and, often, as overwhelming her spouse with her numerous and intimidating forms, so much so that he even tries to flee in fear.[1] In the later Puranas, the

Brihaddharma Purana and Mahabhagavat Purana, Sati assumes the terrible forms of Kali or Chhinnamasta and scares Shiva into allowing her to go to the yajna.

Sati's visit to her paternal home resonates in practices associated with married women in Hindu society. The cult of the goddess Nandadevi of the Garhwal area in Uttaranchal, for instance, illustrates the potential danger posed by unfairly restricting a woman's freedom to return to her native village, that is, her father's domain. Every September an annual pilgrimage wends its way through many local villages where Nandadevi is worshipped, symbolizing her return to her native village. It is believed that if the pilgrimage is not undertaken, the goddess gets offended for she assumes that she is no longer loved and respected in her own home. Such implied neglect or indifference will court her wrath. Although Garhwali literature stresses that a woman is totally transformed when she marries because she becomes part of her husband's lineage, the women believe that they are strongly identified with, influenced by and related to their family's village, their maits. The bride who has gone away should continue to be respected and must be invited back to the village for all its important festivals and events.[2] Both men and women share the belief that a woman has the ability to effectively curse her husband or father if this is not done.

By some quirk the practice of a widow killing herself on her husband's funeral pyre has come to be termed 'sati' through association with the myth of Sati 'burning' herself, though the latter was in no way connected to the death of a spouse. Although some myths do describe Sati jumping into the sacrificial fire, self-immolation is more frequently referred to. Some versions also mention that Sati resorted to burning herself with her own fire when the sacrificial fire refused to touch her.

In Hinduism flammability is considered a marker of sanctity. There are many episodes in myths where fire is used to 'purify'. For example, in the 'Aranyakanda' of Tulsidas's Ramayana, the sage Sharabhanga, and Shabari, a devout worshipper of Rama, burn themselves in their yogic fire following an overwhelming encounter with Rama. The Puranas tell us that Daksha's cruel behaviour makes Sati feel reviled and increasingly guilty, as though she is responsible for Daksha's verbiage against Shiva and the vilification he is subjected to. Unable to do anything to her father she resorts to the final drastic step of taking her own life by generating her own fire, which will purify her sullied lineage and cleanse her soul of the sin of bringing slander upon her gracious husband.

In the end, Sati's decision to give up her life arises from her failure to reconcile the opposing paths of her father and her husband, the paths of ritual sacrifice and ascetic detachment, pravritti and nivritti (see 'Daksha'). She tries to explain to her father the goodness she can see in Shiva and the importance of understanding his way of life and gives up only when she realizes the futility of her effort. So great is the predicament of attempting a rapprochement that ultimately she has to 'sacrifice' her life so that truth may prevail.

❦ Daksha ❦

In the beginning of time, when Brahma was creating the universe, ten Prajapatis emerged from his fecund and meditating mind. From these glorious progenitors, in turn, human beings have descended. They are the fathers of the human race, the Prajapatis—Marichi, Atri, Angiras, Pulastya, Pulaha, Kratu, Vashishtha, Bhrigu, Narada, and I, Daksha.

I am Daksha. I am the skilful one, the ultimate brahman, the perfect, impeccable priest.

There was a time when I was considered a fanatic for precision, but I never took umbrage to such comments. My steadfast belief in the sanctity and necessity of ritual and the years I had dedicated to attaining perfection in the performance of rites led me to be nominated the keeper of customs and traditions, the upholder of law and authority. It was a responsibility of utmost gravity and I tried at all times to conduct myself with the decorum, poise and honour that my position demanded. Not for me the escapades, romps and shenanigans of certain gods, goddesses and godlings. To their devotees, they may have seemed utterly charming in their tomfoolery and comical ways, but their constant floundering and remarkable ability to get entangled in the most bizarre situations aroused nothing but contempt in me. Why did mortals pray to these buffoons for protection and miracles? In my pursuit of perfection I turned to my yajnas and removed from my mind the thought of those gods. It is not enough to simply perform sacrifices, but to perform them in honour of those who are worthy of elaborate rituals. I had neither time nor leisure to waste on frivolous pastimes or other mundane matters. I satisfied my soul with the meticulous planning required for flawless sacrifices and ceremonies. For what is more important in the world than ritual and ceremony and procedures that establish order? The yajna is, after all, within its sanctified space, a microcosm of the universe.

On my part, I was deeply involved in every stage of preparation. Every task, every detail of the groundwork, however tedious, had to bear my seal of approval. From the larger tasks of identifying an auspicious hour from astronomical settings, preparing the sacrificial ground, constructing the altar, and gathering and arranging for the offerings and oblations, to the minutest detail of baking the sacrificial cakes of rice, flour and ghee, sanctifying the durba grass by means of mantras, even supervising the crafting of the utensils and ladles to be used in the yajna— every bit of it was within my purview. It is I who inspired the hotr, the udgatr and the adhvaryu to display their expertise at their individual functions and duties. The hotrs who presided over my ceremonies recited the richas, the verses from the Rig Veda, like none other. The udgatrs were unmatched in the singing of melodies from the Sama Veda. The adhvaryus were meticulous in their knowledge of the sacrificial formulae set down in the Yajur Veda.

The sweet fragrance of incense, the heat from the fire, the billowing smoke, the tears streaming down, the rich smell of burning ghee and the entrancing chants enlivened my senses. I thrived on the successful performance of a yajna. It was my opinion that nothing could consolidate the world more effectively than the tradition of ritual. Love, affection, contemplation—who had time for such trivialities? Such things were meant for the unintelligent, those incapable of mastering the art of detailed precision. As far as I was concerned, yajna was life, yajna was the universe, yajna was everything.

My fame having spread far and wide, the best and the brightest of the celestial world attended the ceremonies I conducted. How could it be that the great Daksha invite them and they don't respond? I never let the presence of the great gods and sages overwhelm me—such feelings are for ordinary beings and I am no ordinary person. Nor did I have a cavalier attitude towards the rituals, even though they were part of my daily existence. Sometimes a ceremony would extend over days and I would cringe at the sight of my esteemed, erudite guests succumbing to slumber even as the offerings were being made. Did they have no respect for these rites? Surely they didn't believe that this was the appropriate time and occasion to catch up on their sleep! Did they think such blatant disregard for tradition would escape my eyes? I usually stayed up many nights before an event agonizing over the last detail, yet I would never be the one nodding off, or smiling foolishly at others, or constantly shifting around as though there were ants tickling my bottom! But then, I was an exception, and it was my penchant for perfection that received unequivocal praise. Jealousy, of course, may lead many of my detractors to accuse me of being unnecessarily surly and pedantic, but I was satisfied with my life, so what cared I about petty people who proclaimed me unduly proud and haughty? I had every right to be.

Only one aspect of my life had the capacity to make me feel vulnerable and distract me from my work. I had fathered sixty daughters who had reached marriageable age in the blink of an eye. Quite immune to their daily chatter—mostly needless laughter and girly quarrels—I was hardly involved in their lives when they were children. Suddenly one day I found my wife, Prasuti, reminding me that they had turned into young women and it was time for us to start looking around for suitable men to be their grooms! Listening to her, my shoulders suddenly felt heavy with the burden of being the father of sixty daughters. I realized that any inadvertent slip on my part on this count could result in a life full of woe for one of my own blood, but I shuddered even more at the thought of becoming a laughing stock among my peers if I made a blunder of such an important task.

There was no place for compromise in this matter. The men I would choose for my daughters were to be my sons-in-law; their names would be associated with mine for life. I spent sleepless nights tossing and turning, and busy days poring over birth charts and consulting my father Brahma. My ideal of perfection constantly interfered with every individual under consideration, and I pondered relentlessly over each match. Only men of calibre, capable of discussing law and custom, wise enough to understand my need for perfection and man enough to emulate all that I represented would be fit to be my sons-in-law. By and by, I was able to single out the men who would now become a part of my family—Kashyapa, Angiras, Bhrigu, Atri, Vashishtha, Pulastya, Pulaha, Kratu and so forth, luminaries all, eminent seers, practitioners, theoreticians of sacrifice, counsellors of kings—and fifty-nine weddings were celebrated with grandeur and opulence to match my eminence.

Yes, fifty-nine weddings—for the youngest, most beloved of my daughters, Sati, had sprung a nasty surprise on me that I had not anticipated.

From her childhood, Sati had been different from my other daughters. Much too restrained and serene for one of her age, she preferred to roam the gardens on her own, even as her sisters gathered together to exclaim over clothes and jewellery. Even when I held the grandest of sacrifices, she would stand around uninterested and unimpressed. Nothing could keep her indoors for too long. Often I chanced upon her gazing out of the window at the blue mountains beyond, completely absorbed in her thoughts, such as I had never seen in someone so young. Yet, while she seemed almost indifferent to what was going on in the household, Sati never shied away from expressing her opinions. She was the only one of my children with whom I could engage in prolonged debates on matters of philosophy and ritual. The others kept a safe distance from me, as daughters should. And there was something else—Sati possessed an inexplicable quality, what one can perhaps call 'goodness'—not in following the rules of the household but just in being herself, doing what she thought was correct. Watching her grow up, I often silently congratulated her mother for bringing up a child with such strong values and a sense of purpose. (There is no point in openly appreciating a wife, for she will take it to heart and strut around uselessly and immediately make a blunder that will ruin all the previous good she has done.) I knew as I watched Sati that finding an apt groom for her would be a difficult task. After all, one of the main conditions for a happy and successful marriage is that the husband should be superior to the wife in every way. But how many men could be Sati's equal, let alone superior to her? I shelved the disquieting strain of thought in full knowledge that one day it would return to haunt me.

At times, however, Sati's inward absorption nettled me. Her face often reflected a lofty sadness that I could not comprehend and some of her actions were quite contrary to my liking. I had heard from the servants that she wandered about the countryside playing with wild animals or even talking and laughing with humble peasants. Though they found this endearing, I found it appalling that rank and position meant little to her. Did she not realize she was a brahman's daughter? Was she not aware of her impeccable lineage? Where was the need for her to fraternize and laugh so gaily with those of the lesser varnas? I often wondered what they talked about, but it did not befit my status to spy on my daughter by asking others about her daily activities. So I tried not to let it bother me. Prasuti too was of no help. The few times I tried broaching the topic, she feigned complete ignorance and told me I was imagining things. It was almost as though she was in denial of this vexatious trait in our daughter.

My worst fears came true when one day Sati approached me and in even tones declared, 'Father, I would like to marry Shiva.' I was taken aback, to say the least. She had said it just like that, with no preliminary humming and hawing, no clumsy words or awkwardness. Why, it was almost a command! I tried not to believe what I had heard. My lovely, delicate Sati was telling me that she wanted to spend her life with that unclean, uncivilized outcaste Shiva!

How could Sati betray me like this? I had never understood what my peers, or everyone else including the gods for that matter, found so mesmerizing about Shiva. If Shiva was indeed a god, why did he go about dressed like a beggar? Pashupati—that is what his followers called him! But of course he was the lord of animals, for was he not an animal himself? What did he know about rituals? Did he even understand the importance of sacrifice? Did Shiva really think his ascetic denial of the world was a new source of religious power? How could one think of achieving immortality without participating in rituals? From the way he lived his life it was clear that he did not realize the power of sacrifice and of the brahmans who perform them. The role of the priests is, after all, to mediate between gods and mortals. We were the gods on earth.

In fact, Shiva even had the audacity to transgress the discipline of the varnas and preach heretical doctrines. All those black-faced skull carriers, liquor addicts, pretas and pishachas who were so devoted to him were beyond the pale of refined breeding. The more I thought about him, the more infuriated I became. Every time I closed my eyes I saw Shiva, his body smeared with ash from the cremation grounds instead of sandalwood paste and adorned with garlands of human bones, sitting in an intoxicated stupor, surrounded by spirits and goblins, his unruly locks covering his shoulders. What was he good for but wandering nude among funeral pyres, laughing and crying like a madman? He had neither courage nor knowledge, for both had fled from him.

And what about the time he had insulted me before all the gods and sages? In a world where I was so highly respected that most people hesitated to look me in the eyes, Shiva had had the audacity to slight me. If I entered a sacrificial ceremony after everyone had been seated, everybody present (except Brahma, of course, for he is my father) rose to their feet to greet me with due respect, but on this particular instance there was one more exception— Shiva. Who was he to ignore what the shrutis laid down and dishonour me? There were many who came to his defence and explained away this unpardonable sin as an oversight on his part. They had the gall to suggest that Shiva's characteristic absentmindedness had led him to appear so insolent. But I was in no mood to listen to such drivel and cursed him and his followers roundly. 'You are not fit to be worshipped or to receive offerings at sacrificial ceremonies,' I said. 'Here on you will be denied sacrificial offerings and be excluded from the prayers and chants in the Vedas. As for those good-for-nothings who hover around you all the time, they will all be reborn as shudras, with no respect in civilized society.'

Still he did not think me important enough to ask for forgiveness for his impudence! It was as if the abuses I hurled at him had not reached his ears. Such was his haughtiness, so aggravating his nonchalance. 'His mind seems to be on bigger things,' claimed his useless supporters, but to me an insult was an insult, and I was not about to forget this one. And now my daughter was telling me he was to be a part of my family!

I tried to reason with Sati, to appeal to her as her father and well-wisher, to coax, cajole and even threaten her, but she was adamant. No amount of dissuasion would change her mind, and when Brahma, my father, approached me with the request not to stand in her way, I was left with no option but to give in.

When the day of the wedding arrived and I saw Shiva and Sati together, I could feel revulsion rising in me. Cloaked in the stench of funeral pyres, bedecked with bones, Shiva looked worse than an ordinary tribal. He was the very antithesis of everything that I had desired for Sati. Moreover, what a din those malformed friends of his were creating. Beating their drums, clapping, dancing around in naked ecstasy, some beady-eyed, some red-eyed, some mere skeletons with grinning countenances, many laughing uproariously baring their ugly stained teeth, displaying their outrageous glee, now that their lord was getting married. Such a distasteful exhibition of emotions! Where was the sophistication of restraint, where was the refinement of understatement? By now I was seething. I

could feel a churning in my stomach and swallowed hard
to suppress the surges of nausea.

There he was now, taking Sati's hand in his. Sati
herself looked strange, different from her usual self. What
had come over her? Had she taken on Shiva's dark colour?
To my amazement I realized she looked pathetically in
love. That is why she looked different. Her eyes were
bright, radiating happiness. Her hair was somewhat
dishevelled, her breath came too fast, her mouth was
half open—I looked away. I could not bear to be a witness
to such shameless display. I gnashed my teeth in anger
and nearly yelled at Prasuti, 'Sati is wicked, disobedient
and rebellious! This is your fault. You are completely
responsible for spoiling her, giving in to all her whims
and fancies since she was a child, and see how we have
had to give in to this horrific one as well.' In the end, I
blocked my mind from the proceedings and mechanically
went about my present duty—greeting the guests and
ensuring they were properly attended to.

Yet, my thoughts would not let me rest. What was
so special about this wretched Shiva that Sati had become
so entranced? He moved about on an old bull that ambled
along as though it had nowhere to go and the only wealth
he had to his name was a skull bowl in which he collected
alms. He had no respect for the codes of civilization and
the hierarchies of society. By choosing him my daughter
had chosen a separate dharma. I did not need to care
about her future any more. To me she had become like

the pot that had fallen into the hands of a chandala. Neither she nor her spouse would ever receive any respect from me.

Since it was beyond my power to stop anything now, all I could do was to move a step back when Sati bent down to touch my feet. I was incapable of giving her my blessings. All the grace, all the affection had been snuffed out of me as quickly as the flame of a candle. I rushed into the inner chambers and bolted the door. I needed to resuscitate myself, to free my mind from the quagmire it was sinking into.

A long time elapsed before I saw Sati again. In my lonely hours, I mourned the loss of my dear daughter as though she were dead. I did not send word to her, nor made any effort to find out how she was adjusting to the harsh life of a beggar's wife. She had caused me a lot of pain. I did not know then that our meeting, when it would finally take place, would have such tragic consequences.

Brahma had, in the meantime, appointed me Prajapati, the chief of all lords of creation. Such an occasion deserved a grand celebration and since I had already performed the Vajapeya ceremony, I decided to host the Brihaspatisava sacrifice, just as the shruti dictates. I chose a place of unmeasured splendour in the holy Naimisha forest in Haridwar as the venue. I commissioned eighty-eight thousand priests to proffer offerings, sixty thousand sages and saints to chant the mantras and another sixty

thousand rishis as choristers. Four priests were assigned
the responsibility of building the altar. Shaunaka and other
leading sages were to perform the yajna, with Vashishtha
as the hotr, Angiras as the adhvaryu, Brihaspati as the
udgatr and Narada as the brahman.

I had invited all the elements from every corner of the
universe to attend the great sacrifice. The clouds and the
mountains, rivers and oceans, creepers and herbs, arrived
in all their glory as did the inhabitants of the upper
regions—the yakshas and suparnas. Then came the
denizens of the depths, the demons and the magnificent
serpent kings and queens, to partake of their share of the
feast. The kings of the earth arrived in state with their
sons, followed by their counsellors and troops. The gods
flocked to my mansion with their wives and offspring in
their shiny gilded chariots. My daughters too arrived
in all their finery, accompanied by their honourable
spouses. Prasuti had told me how excited the girls were
to return home to their parents and childhood friends.
They chattered busily, admiring each other's clothes
and jewellery, discussing the invitees, greeting old
acquaintances. Just as the oblations were being offered
to the fire to mark the commencement of the sacrifice,
the Vasus, the twelve Adityas, two Ashvins, the Maruts
and fourteen Manus also entered the premises. Vishnu
himself took charge of overseeing the event. The grounds
reverberated with the apsaras singing to the rich tunes
and sounds of flutes and lutes, and as the sacrifice

proceeded, the devas were invoked to receive their respective shares.

There was only one god whom I had not cared to invite to the ceremony; nor had I arranged for offerings to be made to him. This was Shiva. Contaminated by association, my daughter Sati too had not qualified to be part of the sacrifice.

Noticing Shankara's absence where the entire host of devas were enjoying their supremacy, the sage Dadhicha asked me, 'How is it that Maheshwara is not being worshipped—Maheshwara, the lord at whose behest everyone from Brahma to the pishachas goes about their tasks?'

I replied, 'Have you not noticed, O great one, that no share is allotted to Rudra in any yajna? Do you not find it astonishing? If indeed he was the greatest god, there would be mantras invoking him and his wife in the scriptures. Shiva has spread confusion among worshippers through his strange ways. Is he an ascetic or does he have a spouse? No one seems to be sure.'

After a moment of silence the knowledgeable sage laughed at me derisively and said (loudly enough for the entire gathering to hear), 'But he is known as Parameshwara, the soul of the universe. He is the one from whom everything derives.'

Determined to prove my point, I said, 'Indeed he is not Parameshwara, the benefactor, but Rudra, the annihilator. He is Hara and embodies only tamas, the darkness of ignorance and destruction. He is the naked mendicant holding a skull. It is not proper to call him the soul of the universe. What is this serpent-slinging, ash-smeared Shiva but the proud abolisher of rites and demolisher of barriers? He teaches the word of the Veda to the shudras, the lowest of the low. He pretends to be auspicious, while in reality he is ashiva. Hence Bhava, the lowest of the gods, never receives any portion of the oblations at any sacrifice, like the gods Indra, Upendra and others do.'

Dadhicha drew a long breath, as though trying to contain his anger, and continued, 'Rudra is the sole annihilator of worlds. He is Paramaheshwara in the form of Kala. It is to him that the righteous scholars, the expounders of the Brahman, pray. Shiva, the great god, witnesses everything, he is the creator of the universe and the embodiment of the Vedas. He is eulogized by the singers of the Sama hymns, the hotrs and the adhvaryus. He is the kind-hearted Hara, the blue-necked Neelakantha. Can you not recognize the lord of a thousand rays?'

I was appalled at this gross misinformation and corrected him, saying, 'The twelve Adityas have come here as sharers in the yajnas. All of them should be known as suns, there is no other.' At this a crescendo of voices rose across the room as, at first hesitant and then gathering confidence, Bhaga, Pushan and many of the others joined me in denigrating Shiva's appalling ways.

Dadhicha watched us in silence and when the din had died down he said in a grave voice, 'There is no doubt that a man incurs great sin in worshipping one who is not worthy of worship and in not worshipping those who deserve to be revered. The punishment meted out by divine intercession is sudden and terrible in that place where evil is received well and good is slighted.' Saying this, he cursed those who had come forward in my support and expressed their anger towards Shiva. His voice shaking with emotion, Dadhicha said, 'You, who have dared to exclude the Supreme Lord from the Vedas, your learning is false, your conduct of life is false. It is you, who are antagonistic to Ishwara, who will be excluded from all Vedic rituals. You boast about your false knowledge. You will be forced to abandon your power of penance and go to naraka. Even though you will then wish to take refuge in him, Hrishikesha will turn his face away from you.'

A sudden, unusual hush had descended on the hall. Puzzled, I looked around and was surprised to find Sati approaching me. This was most unexpected. Why was she here? Had she not realized why I had not sent her an invitation? She looked troubled and weary, but I was not about to give in to useless sentiments. She had put me through enough pain and humiliation, what was she here to do now?

I tried to ignore her, and had turned away to continue my argument with Dadhicha, when she addressed me directly. 'Oh Daksha, dear father,' she said, 'Brahma's entire creation has been invited here, to be honoured by you with gifts and attendants. But my revered husband alone is not a part of this magnificent affair. All this appears to me to be a void without him. In all probability you have forgotten him…'

Earlier, when Sati had expressed her desire to marry Shiva, I had merely tried to reason her out of it and pointed out how different her life would be in Shiva's domain. But hatred needs no dry embers, it burns of its own volition. And now, already incensed by Dadhicha's words, I told Sati exactly what I thought of her precious husband and how much shame it brought me to be associated with him.

In the midst of my ranting, Sati cut me off and in a flash I recognized the humiliation and anger in her eyes. But what was this she was telling me? Was this the daughter I was so proud of at one time? Was she now expounding on Shiva's greatness and the virtues that he so obviously did not possess? Was she instructing me on karma and the siddhis and condemning *my* way of life?

Yet, as she spoke I noticed a note of resignation creeping into her voice, as though she knew that Shiva and I would never see eye to eye, never connect with each other as she wished we would. I suddenly regretted my inability to recognize earlier her steadfast and complete love for Shiva. Her resigned look gradually turned into one of determination and finally an alarming calm transformed my daughter's face. I watched in horror as Sati, my dearest daughter, the child I had played with in my lap, who at one time had been the apple of my eye, cursed her birth in my home and set herself ablaze. Oh ruin! Utter and total ruin! My daughter gone, my grand sacrifice polluted! It seemed at that moment that the worst fate had befallen me, that I was witnessing naraka right there at the sacred venue. I did not realize that this was just a preview of the horror that was to be wreaked on us in a few moments. A sob arose in my throat at the waste of it all, my daughter's life, my arrogance, my harsh words. Completely spent in spirit and body, I fell in a heap on the floor.

My guests had so far watched the proceedings in alarm and silence, but now they seemed agitated and afraid. Some of them were pointing to the north and when I sat up and looked around I noticed a cloud of dust rapidly making its way towards us. The priests and the other members of the sacrificial assembly shook in terror. 'What darkness is this?' they asked. 'Winds are not blowing, nor can these be robbers. Cows are not driven home so hastily. From where has this dust arisen? Is the world readying itself for pralaya?'

Before I knew it chaos had ensued as the guests ran helter-skelter, screaming for help, tripping and toppling over each other in their hurry to escape. Then I saw him: A gargantuan creature, with a thousand heads, a thousand eyes, and huge arms, also a thousand in number. In each

hand he held terrifying weapons and he was smeared
with ash from head to toe. Raising his trident, which
was capable of killing even the god of death, he dashed
forth, the ornaments on his feet jingling with each stride.
He roared mightily, exposing his curved, bloody fangs.
His blood-shot eyes darted around, glowing with fury,
resembling the fires at the close of the yugas. As I rose
slowly to my feet, trying to fathom the scene unfolding
before me, Pushan whispered hoarsely into my ear,
'That is Virabhadra! Created from a single strand of
Rudra's locks!'

Then hordes of terrifying creatures, all followers
of Rudra, rushed in from all sides of the sacrificial
pandal with weapons in their hands. They were short
and dark, with faces and bellies like a crocodile's.
Virabhadra created more soldiers from the pores of
his skin—the Romajas. Riding astride their bulls,
accompanied by wives more terrible in form, they
surrounded Virabhadra. Together they set about
destroying my prized sacrifice, terrorizing the priests and
their wives and attacking the rishis and seers. Even the
gods were not spared. Those trying to flee were captured
and devoured. Yama's staff was split in two and Indra
lay trodden on and groaning. Wielding their tridents and
iron clubs, the demons made the ten quarters reverberate
with their shouts of victory. A terrible smile broke on
Virabhadra's lips as he turned his attention to me and
said: 'We are the followers of Sharva, the immeasurable

brilliance. We have come here to claim our share of the sacrifice.'

I retreated in horror but he caught me in a deathly grip and lifted me high in the air. Then, throwing me down on the floor and seating himself on my chest, he raised a sharp-edged weapon to severe my head, just like he would for a sacrificial animal. The last thing I heard before darkness descended over my eyes was a triumphant shout from the bhutas, pretas and pishachas, who had loved every minute of the mayhem.

I have now awakened, as though from a deep sleep. Answering my wife's pleas, the gracious Ashutosha, has restored my life and replaced my missing head with a goat's.

Just as I have returned in body and mind, my soul too has experienced an epiphany. Gone is the darkness that had shrouded my vision. Therein has vanished avidya, therein has vanished ego, therein has vanished false pride. I know now that rituals alone cannot lead to salvation; there has to be contemplation, there has to be consideration, there has to be forgiveness. For the priceless wisdom I have gained, I am grateful. I am the wretched soul for not realizing the truth, for putting my daughter through such misery, for not comprehending her love for Shiva. I am the poorer for it, for not only have I proved my unworthiness to mortals and immortals but I have also lost my dearest child.

I bow to thee, Shiva, as I hear the sound of your praises. Never will I conduct another sacrifice without first worshipping you. Never will I think that my form of worship is superior to the path your devotees follow. Let them smear their bodies with ash. Let them dance wildly. Let them look inward for peace. I have only admiration and awe for their oneness with their lord.

Aum namah Shivaya!

The name Daksha means able, competent and intelligent. Daksha is best known as one of the pre-Vedic Prajapatis, the lords of creation. Later he is referred to as one of the rishis and the son of Brahma, born of his right thumb. His consort is Prasuti and the number of daughters he fathered varies in different texts. On more than one occasion he comes across as an overprotective father.

The story of Shiva's destruction of Daksha's sacrifice is an ancient and popular myth and is, in fact, one of the grandest and most quoted feats ascribed to Shiva in the Puranas. Like many other myths, it embraces Vedic and Puranic antecedents. The germ of the story is found in the Taittiriya Samhita (Yajur Veda) and the main story can be found in the Linga, Kurma, Vayu, Brahma, Matsya, Varaha, Bhagavat, Shiva and Vamana Puranas, with slight variations, and in the Mahabharata and the Ramayana as well. It is also a favourite subject of Hindu sculpture, at least with the Shaivite Hindus, and figures conspicuously both at Elephanta and at Ellora, indicating that the legend of Daksha was popular when the cavern temples were constructed.

The Daksha–Shiva Conflict and What It Represents

The reasons underlying the Daksha–Shiva conflict can be interpreted in many ways and at many levels.

A Personality Conflict

At the simplest level, the mayhem at the sacrificial venue results from an ego tussle between two creators. The Bhagavat Purana attributes the rift between Daksha and Shiva to Daksha's notion that Shiva had insulted him by not acknowledging his presence on one occasion. Reacting to this perceived slight by Shiva, Daksha Prajapati had called Shiva a heretic and a chain of curses followed excluding Shiva from the Vedas, banishing him from heaven and relegating him to the kingdom of ghosts and pishachas. Following this, Prajapati and the gods denied Rudra a share of the sacrifice by simply leaving him out of the ceremony. Infuriated at the insult, Rudra had destroyed the sacrifice, beheaded Daksha, the sacrificer, and sullied the sacrificial fire by throwing his head into it. Alternatively, Shiva's outrage could also be a reaction to the treatment meted out to his wife and her ultimate tragic death.

Sectarian Rivalry

In the Mahabharata and the Vamana Purana an argument between Daksha and Dadhicha over the relative superiority of Vishnu and Shiva leads Daksha to ignore Shiva while planning a grand sacrifice to Vishnu. Again, the Kurma Purana has Daksha saying, 'All he [Shiva] manages to do is further confuse the hapless, beleaguered, stupid worshipper who is ready to follow anything and I was not prejudiced just because Vishnu was my patron.' So it may equally indicate a struggle between the followers of Vishnu, represented by Daksha, and those of Shiva—in which at first the former but finally the latter acquire victory.

Pravritti and Nivritti: The Reconciliation

Essentially, the Daksha–Shiva opposition is seen to represent the conflict between pravritti dharma, characterized by the orthodox sacrificial culture, and nivritti dharma, which emphasizes renunciation and yoga, or between two modes of living—the ascetic (Shiva) and the householder (Daksha).

An idea of the concepts of pravritti and nivritti, which Daksha and Shiva respectively represent, is crucial to a proper understanding of this conflict and, indeed, to much of Hinduism itself.

Shankaracharya, the great Hindu theologian of the eighth century CE, talked about a twofold Vedic religion. After the universe was created, Brahma, wishing to secure order in it, first created the Prajapatis and caused them to adopt pravritti dharma, that is, engaging in worldly activity in order to maintain the ever-revolving wheel of samsara by performing actions in accordance with the scriptures or executing actions that deserve to be performed for increased material satisfaction. He then created the renunciants and caused them to adopt the nivritti dharma, the religion of renunciation characterized by wisdom and indifference to worldly objects, involving activities that are free of desire and founded on knowledge.

Pravritti dharma includes the particularly powerful sexual desire, the foundation of the family. The family itself is the centre of an individual's social complex of relationships and far-ranging activities such as different kinds of rituals, including the sacrifices that are referred to at length in this chapter. Pravritti as a whole is driven by desire of many kinds—for wealth, for pleasure, for the approval of others, or even to please the gods—and has long been practised by all castes and religious orders in the Hindu varnashrama. Nivritti, on the other hand, involves an inward withdrawal in order to attain liberation from samsara.

This dualistic–dialectic divide in religion, as a way of life and an ontology of participation, maintains order in the universe. The ashrama system is an attempt to reconcile this conflicting trend within Hinduism. Thus, the first two stages of life—that of the student and, more specifically, the householder—represent the phase of participation in worldly activities, while the later stages of the hermit and the renunciant represent withdrawal from them. This is an instance of the 'middle path' of Hinduism, as it were, the path between complete immersion in worldly activities and abject withdrawal.

The case of Yajnavalkya in the Brihadaranyaka Upanishad provides the best example of this (see 'Parvati'). The Bhagavad Gita combines the two concepts and advises on how one could be involved in a variant strand of pravritti: a discipline where one engages in social activity while combining it with asceticism, thus elevating and enriching both. Thus asceticism becomes more than mere abstinence and everyday activity is not tied up with self-seeking motives. In this manner, the path of action comes to lay the same emphasis on renunciation as the path of sanyasa does.

Shiva's mythology is interpreted to represent this dual paradox in Hindu tradition, as he is portrayed as being involved in both forces as a householder and as a mahayogi. The renouncer and the enjoyer are inextricably woven in Shiva's personality.

The challenges Shiva faces as a householder are dealt with in the chapter 'Parvati', but the different facets of asceticism that he manifests deserve equal attention.

Asceticism, basically the detachment from the material world leading to spiritual transformation, is an ancient path of wisdom and transcendence.

In historical terms, asceticism manifested itself sometime around the sixth century BCE in India, specifically taking shape along the mid-Gangetic plain. The first inscriptional evidence, which can be positively dated, is an Ashokan inscription dating back to the fourth century BCE. However, the trajectory of the concept of asceticism in India can be traced through an ancestry of thought and behaviour going back to the Keshins and Vratyas who find mention in Vedic literature.

The idea of renunciation, conjoined with asceticism, was of low priority in brahmanic thought until the time of the Upanishads. In the Upanishads we find the earliest references to practices that were later related to asceticism. The traditional Vedic world view was world-affirming and not world-negating, essentially praising the householder's life, that is, marriage, earning wealth and begetting children, and brahman priests themselves were rarely given to renunciation.

In the Upanishads we already find a section of people who may very well have been from within the brahmanical tradition but who were disenchanted with the world of ritual, among other things. They voluntarily separated themselves from it, living in forest hermitages in order to seek the ultimate truth. There is mention of the homeless and we hear about their wanderings; sometimes they are organized in monastic establishments. Lay donors and royal patrons were important to them. In fact, later texts clearly reveal that asceticism was a radical departure from and often in conflict with the orthodox brahmanical socio-religious system. Suggesting a strikingly different religious orientation from that found in the Vedas, a passage in the Brihadaranyaka Upanishad (4.4.22) states that the ancient rishis or seers—those who forsook the world and realized Brahman (the Absolute)—'rose above the desire for sons and the desire for wealth and the desire for worlds, and lived the life of a wandering mendicant.'

However, the earliest reference to what appears to be Shaiva ascetics is found in a hymn in the Rig Veda. Recently translated by scholars, this is the powerful 'Keshisukta' which describes silent and long-haired people who, through their inward concentration, attain enlightenment. This can be seen as a precursor to the idea of the ascetic's search for gnosis. Even though the ascetic is a very minor religious type in the early Vedic period, this description marks the beginning of a thought process.

He with the long loose locks supports Agni, and moisture, heaven and earth:
He is all sky to look upon: he with long hair is called this light.

The Munis, girdled with the wind, wear garments soiled of yellow hue.
They, following the wind's swift course, go where the Gods have gone before.

Transported with our Munihood we have pressed on into the winds:
You therefore, mortal men, behold our bodies and no more.

The Muni, made associate in the holy work of every God,
Looking upon all varied forms flies through the region of the air.

The Steed of Vata, Vayu's friend, the Muni, by the Gods impelled,
In both the oceans hath his home, in eastern and in western sea.

Treading the path of sylvan beasts Gandharvas and Apsaras,
He with long locks, who knows the wish, is a sweet, most
    delightful friend.

Vayu hath churned for him: for him he poundeth things most
    hard to bend,
When he with long loose locks hath drunk, with Rudra,
    water from the cup.[1]

    The hymn describes a 'muni', a word which in later literature is applied to a holy person or ascetic, and refers to other features—such as long hair, the practice of silence (mauna), nakedness, bodies smeared with mud or possibly ash, or covered with soiled rags—which could all describe a Shaiva yogi in India today. The verse mentions the Keshin ('long-haired one') drinking 'vish', which later came to mean poison, prepared in the company of Rudra. This suggests the ritual use of intoxicants that induce the kind of frenzied behaviour associated with reaching a state of ecstasy. In the second verse, the munis are referred to as 'vatavasanah' ('girdled with the wind'), possibly a reference to their nakedness, and their clothes, if they do wear any, are 'malah' ('garments soiled of yellow hue'). They are possibly possessed by gods and display the ability to read minds, a power attributed to accomplished yogis in later yoga traditions. We are also told that the muni 'supports Agni'; perhaps once the muni gives up the domestic fires, he internalizes the heat generated by austerities. Such features are clearly antithetical to the rituals of conventional Vedic religion and have great similarity to shamanic practices and experiences found in other cultures.

The Rig Veda mentions another group of ascetics called the Yatis, or ascetics who could 'control their passions'. The Atharva Veda and a few other texts mention Yatis being killed by Indra. It is not clear whether they were non-Aryan ascetics or a group of dissenters from the orthodox brahmanical religion.

Some early Vedic texts also mention a more obscure group of ascetics called the Vratyas. In the Panchavimsha Brahmana (17.4.1), they are described as 'shamanichamedhra' or 'those whose penises hang low through control of passion'.[2] Book 15 of the Atharva Veda contains references to Vratyas, but here they are a community of aggressive warriors who move about in bands. It is said that they live on the edges of Aryan society and may have been connected to the Keshins. They are described as being dressed in black, with two ram skins, one white, one black, slung over their shoulders. They wear turbans and their insignia are their sharp, pointed sticks, an ornament around their necks ('nishka') and an unstrung bow.

The Vratyas, who were concentrated in the northeast of India, spoke the same language as the Vedic people but were regarded with disdain by them. They wandered from place to place practising austerities, including standing erect for one year without moving. Since they are mentioned with opprobrium, they may have been non-Aryan priests of non-Vedic fertility rites, or even forerunners of the yogi, the fakir or the wandering mendicant. Rudra is sometimes referred to as 'Vratyapati', or the father of the Vratyas, and in the Mahabharata all Shaivite ascetics are referred to as Vratyas.[3]

A few points about the Vratyas delineated in the texts reveal the possible connection to Shaiva sects in subsequent periods. Chief among these are the mahavrata and the rites connected to fertility. Hymns were chanted for the entire duration of the rituals and, most interesting of all, they included varying cycles of inhalation and exhalation, a very important feature of pranayama, which is practised even today. Sexual intercourse and obscene language, additional features of the rituals, resonate later in Shaiva-Tantric cults. In these descriptions the Vratyas appear as a group of shamans moving towards ascetic or yogic practices. This could have arisen from nostalgia for the nomadic state, or it could indicate a flouting of growing authoritarianism in a society in which stable agricultural settlements were becoming the norm and wanderers were disapproved of.

Interestingly enough, there is mention of a special purification ritual, the Vratyashtoma, by which the Vratyas, considered outsiders, could be assimilated into Vedic society to assume the Aryan status which they had forfeited by not undertaking the brahmanical rites of passage.

Initially proponents of asceticism believed that tapas and dhyana were more effective than rituals of sacrifice in helping the devotee to reach a state of bliss, but gradually absolute freedom of the soul came to be considered as the desirable path for achieving a state of ecstasy or ananda. This, then, justified the activities of Shaiva ascetics like the Pashupatas and other more extreme sects who courted 'freedom' by all kinds of antisocial means. Not surprisingly, the brahman community resisted the ascetic tradition. They considered it a threat to their order because it stressed on personal autonomy and marked a definite shift from the varna structure. Yet a compromise is arrived at with Shiva entering the fold of sacrifices, and at a social level through the ashrama system where asceticism gets accommodated in the third and fourth stages of the life cycle.

Orthodoxy vs the Nonconformist

Rudra-Shiva has been traditionally excluded from Vedic sacrifice. That Rudra did not conform to the ideal of an Aryan god is proved by a number of concurrent testimonies. The Mahabharata frequently refers to his seizing the property of other gods. Most despicable in brahmanical eyes, Shiva hobnobs with beings such as ganas, bhutas, Kiratas and Nishadas (both tribes that the Aryans despised), rogues, robbers and cheats. In the 'Sabha Parva' of the Mahabharata, Jarasandha contemplates appeasing Rudra with human offerings and later literature depicts in no uncertain terms the anti-Vedic propensities of the followers of Shiva. His wife, Parvati, is also not painted in very attractive colours; neither are her attendants and associates, many of whom belong to tribes despised by Aryan society— the Shabaras, Varavaras and Pulindas.

The Bhagavat Purana has an elaborate version of the story of Daksha's sacrifice which shows how Shiva was viewed by followers of other religious sects. The Puranas were sectarian, each one authored by either Shakta, Shaiva or Vaishnava followers, and hence propagated the might and the goodness of particular deities as compared to others and preached the efficacy of worshipping them. The myths were mutated to place the particular god at centre stage. The author of the Bhagavat Purana, no doubt a devout Vaishnava, has Daksha describing Shiva as monkey-eyed, given to roaming in the cremation grounds with his attendants, ghosts and goblins, the impure and the 'riteless', sometimes laughing and at other times crying. His naked body is smeared with ashes from funeral pyres and he has matted locks on his head. He wears bones and a garland of skulls as ornaments. Yet, in the same text, we also have Nandishwara, a supporter of Shiva, vehemently criticizing the Vedic way of life, just like Dadhicha in the Mahabharata. It is interesting that the composite Rudra-Shiva's basic features are composed of a blend of Vedic and anti-Vedic elements, a wonderful example of early assimilation of ideas and peoples. Such instances clearly suggest that the Vedic 'Rudra' was fused with the 'Shiva' of the Puranas and the epics.

The persistent tradition of non-Vedic association renders it extremely probable that Rudra was thought of as a 'savage' deity and that his worship was initially considered outlandish. The Vedic Indian looked upon Shiva as a low-class deity and did not offer him any oblations along with Indra and the other gods. There is also enough evidence to suggest that worshippers of Shiva were essentially non-brahman and that brahmans were directed not to worship the phallic symbol.

The Rig Veda heaps opprobrium upon those who worship the phallus. Subsequently, in the Puranas and the epics, all the myths go into lengthy explanations of the popularity of linga worship, indicating the deep unease caused earlier by the phallic symbol.

As a staunch advocate of the orthodox Vedic culture Daksha, therefore, despises Shiva and all that is associated with him. He is described as cursing Nandi and Shiva's other servants and followers as heretics and outcastes and ordering them to stay far away from the world of the Vedas. They are going to be reborn in the Kali age as shudras, he says, because they take pleasure in profane behaviour. Daksha's unease with them reflects the standpoint of society, which attempts to understand and accommodate the wide moral latitude of these celestial beings.

The reluctance to acknowledge Shiva's legitimate divine status finally reached a head in Daksha's magnificent and pompous sacrifice where Shiva was excluded and chaos ensued. Not inviting Shiva to the sacrifice seems like a simple breach of etiquette but it has devastating consequences. Shiva avenges his exclusion, and the form of revenge he chooses is, not surprisingly, a yajna, the definitive symbol of early Vedism.

The epic and Puranic tellings of the myth mark a transition in the trajectory of Hinduism, from a period of religion based on Vedic and upper-class supremacy to a period when it became necessary to recognize the phallic deity and other deified heroes worshipped by people outside the Aryan communities.

It is almost as though the myth provides the raison d'être for the assimilation of Shiva into the brahmanical pantheon. From now on worshippers will no longer be yoked to sacrifice as the only means of salvation. The destruction of Daksha's yajna may in fact be looked upon as the most blatant criticism of ritual sacrifice. What better way to do this than to conjure the elaborate setting of a sacrifice in a myth and have it transformed into a massacre? The myth narrates how Shiva later released Daksha from the sin of dishonouring him by restoring the sacrifice and replacing Daksha's head with that of a goat, but in the end Shiva has terrorized the other gods into worshipping him and sharing the sacrificial offerings with him. The violence with which the yajna is destroyed may be interpreted as Shiva's forcible entry into the Vedic pantheon.

It is said in the Bhagavat Purana that those who are ignorant and think only of the mortal frame hate the lord Shiva. Daksha's intellect is confused by arthavada, that is, aspiration for the acquisition of wealth and possessions, and he is engrossed in karmic rituals pertaining to sacrifices and other such acts. He is attached to the householder's life, which is full of deceptive pseudo-religious practices. This kind of worship amounts to avidya and would lead to a continuous swirling in samsara, the cycle of birth, death and rebirth. With his intellect wrongly concentrated on material wealth and fame, and having forgotten the real nature of the soul, Daksha is as good as a beast. The sacrificial 'beast' must be killed, and the worshipper's nescience should be destroyed along with it.

Only Rudra, the killer par excellence, can simultaneously destroy the sacrifice and perform it in honour of the truth by throwing the beast's head into the fire as an oblation. In his dual role as the destroyer and the creator, Shiva once again mediates between Vedic and non-Vedic views of ritual and resolves the ambivalence of the Vedic myths.

Parvati

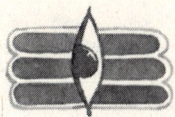

I am Parvati, Shiva's consort.

We are two aspects of the same reality, Shiva and I. I am Shakti, the primal, creative energy, the dynamic aspect of creation. Shiva is static and transcendent, the meditative consciousness. He is being; I am power. We grace life as complements to each other, for life comprises both contemplation and action, like fire and heat or sun and sunshine.

Entire lifetimes spent with Shiva have left me unsatisfied, yearning for more, always more. Like an eternally spinning wheel I return again and again in the cycles of time, to make him mine. In a previous birth as Sati, and now as Parvati, to me it seems the most natural thing to be—in love with Shiva.

I have always dreamed of having the perfect romantic encounter with Shiva. How wonderful it would be if one glance at me could unsettle the mightiest of gods! His brooding eyes would chance upon me as I unmindfully plucked wild mountain flowers to string on my long braid, or made my way to a cool gushing stream for a bath. Then, as I darted away from his sight, he would experience an unexpected, wretched emptiness and realize that his life had no meaning without me by his side. Alas, this was not to be, and I was united with him for a very practical purpose: The gods required our offspring to be born, to help them destroy a demon who had become too unruly for them to handle. Who could they turn to but me; I am Shakti, I am the power that stirs the quiescent one to participate in creation and the enjoyment of created beings.

After I sacrificed my life as Sati, Shiva went through a period of inconsolable grieving. Unable to bear the void Sati had left, he drifted about, miserable, tormented by memories of their time together. It seemed like Shiva's remorse would last for ever. But time is an ever-moving stream—pain like joy gets swept away in its flow—and Shiva, being Kalabhairava himself, gradually abandoned his fierce mourning, retreated to the mountains and immersed himself in tapas once again. With Sati he had grudgingly tasted the sweetness of grihastha, diffidently learned to love and had found bliss where he had never imagined he would—only to have his love brutally snatched away. He had now returned to his self-absorption determined to be impenetrable to all.

While Shiva remained thus absorbed in meditation, refusing to be stirred for millennia on end, destroying anyone or anything that dared disturb him, the gods were suffering unspeakable misery at the hands of the wilful demon, Taraka. The terrifying creature with ten thousand hands had stolen the gods' wives, strangled his enemies, plundered the gem reserves of sea and sky and broken into the celestial homes of the apsaras. Fed up with the shenanigans of the malevolent and mighty asura, the gods approached Brahma for a solution. Brahma informed them rather disconsolately that only one power was capable of rescuing them from the clutches of the destructive Taraka: a son born of the union of Shiva with Shakti. 'A son of Shiva?' the gods inquired, looking more hopeless than ever, for Shiva had no interest in worldly affairs such as marriage, producing offspring and other entanglements that accompanied a connubial state. Glumly they acknowledged that Shiva's inclination to be perpetually wrapped up in himself worked to the utmost disadvantage of the entire universe. But they were in danger of being routed out of the heavens very soon. How long were they to put up with Taraka's oppression before Shiva emerged from his tapas?

So it was that our union was carefully concocted by the gods. They hatched an intricate plan and followed it judiciously. I rendered their first step effortless as I took no time at all to agree to their request to win Shiva's heart, be his bride and bring his offspring into the world. Had I not been waiting, always in love, always ready to take up the challenge of winning over the reclusive ascetic, the reluctant bridegroom Shiva? Had I not been patient enough after my union with him as Sati had ended so cruelly, so abruptly, depriving us of the purnatva of being a couple?

Thus was I born as Parvati, daughter of the mighty Himalaya. I grew up in the mountains—those enticing, dazzling, self-possessed barriers of stone. My very essence was shaped by them. There they stood, stolid, unchanging, free from the shackles of time, exemplifying freedom in their very nature, and always calling out to me. Grandeur for me was the mountains, beauty for me was the mountains, loyalty for me was the mountains. In their shadow I felt secure, I felt protected, I felt one with the universe.

Shiva's opposition to a matrimonial tie was expected. He was after all the Mahayogi, far removed in character and inclination from the humdrum world. When his spirit moved him, he would select a rock, spread his tiger skin on it and, assuming a yogic posture, lapse into the stillest of silences, eyes firmly shut and turned inwards to the core of his mysterious being. His quest seemed to begin and end with himself. The challenge of awakening in him an ananda different from satchidananda, the true yogic bliss that he was accustomed to experiencing, made my task ahead all the more appealing.

Men of all standing, mortal and immortal, have been brought to their knees by feminine charm. The ethereal world boasts of ravishingly beautiful women who have effortlessly enticed gods and destroyed the tapas of many a stern and renowned sage. But, as everyone knew, no such advances had ever affected Shiva. In order to appeal to Shiva, a woman would have to possess much more than physical beauty; complete and unadulterated devotion alone could attract his attention. To make Shiva mine and to communicate my resolve to be his spouse, I thus chose the path most familiar to him: tapas. My path to Shiva was not going to be ordinary or easy, but what did it matter when he would be mine at the end of it?

I meditated with unwavering concentration for three thousand years, my mind firmly fixed on nothing but Shiva. I clothed myself in deer skin and sat through countless eras immersed in meditation. As time became insignificant in the search for truth, I grew insensible to all deprivations, all mortifications of the body. I sat surrounded by fire during the scorching summer, stood on one leg, neck-deep in water, during the rainy season and the harsh winter, and lived on leaves and, sometimes, only air. Wild beasts did not harm me, neither did I fear them. My mind dwelt on one thing only: my union with Shiva and the birth of our offspring who would free the worlds from the terror unleashed by the cursed Taraka.

Even then, my devotion to Shiva was put to the test with annoying regularity. Sages and seers came by trying to dissuade me, saying, 'The trident-bearing Shiva has an inauspicious body. He is naked and ill-featured. He feels no shame at his nakedness and has no home or pedigree. He associates with ghosts and goblins and the like.' I did not feel the need to dignify their petty statements with a verbal response; instead I answered them with a scornful glance, conveying my contempt for their avidya.

Shiva too came to test me, his curiosity kindled by the praises the devas were singing of a maiden who was performing rigorous penance to win his blessings. Appearing before me in the guise of a brahmacharin, Maheshwara said, 'Look at you, you with eyes like the petals of the lotus—and where is that three-eyed creature Shiva? You are moon-faced, he is five-faced. Shiva's birth and pedigree cannot be traced. His caste is not recognized. He has neither learning nor wisdom, nor even knowledge of the enjoyments of a householder. His assistants are ghosts; he holds poison in his throat. You wish to discard your fine garments in order to wear the hide; unmindful of the sunlight, you wish to seek the light of the glow-worm.' I did not so much as flinch at his harsh words. I continued to meditate in silence. As the brahmacharin turned to walk away I looked up and thought I saw a trace of a smile playing on his lips.

Ultimately, when Shiva, satisfied with my tapas, graced me with his presence, and asked me what boon he could grant me, I paid obeisance to him and said, 'O Mahadeva, fulfil the desire of all the gods, fulfil the desire of the whole world, fulfil the desire of my heart and make me your wife.' Shiva acquiesced easily. Perhaps besides being pleased with my single-minded devotion to him, he also felt stirrings of love and desire, as I did. I had yearned to be cherished by Shambhu for so long that I had no qualms born of ego to make me mask it. As he stood before me, my love, raw and unhinged, was as open as the blue skies for all to see.

My parents were curious about Shiva when they learnt he was to be my husband. I tried to explain to them what he meant to me and to the rest of the universe, but I was at a loss for words. To merely describe Shiva can never define him. He is the eternal, the unmanifest and therefore indefinable. You can sense him, you can feel him, but how do you convey him through mere words? Finally I said, 'Shiva is abundance, wholeness personified. However much one takes from him, still more remains.' I was not sure whether they agreed with me or even understood what I was saying, but my parents were gracious enough to accept our union without questioning me further.

And so Shiva and I were united. For thousands of years our love-making caused the earth to tremble. What was this magic that would not allow me to be sated? I was mesmerized by Shiva's eyes that never left mine, snaring my gaze, even as he proceeded to gently take off my jewellery. Slowly, patiently, almost deferentially, he removed the ornaments that would poke him while we made love, while those that did not come in the way were allowed to stay. By now my curiosity had got the better of my shyness and I would look into his eyes, desperately trying to read his mind. Instead of savouring the moment, relishing his touch and his absorption in me, churlish suspicions surfaced in the sea of my thoughts. How did he possess such expertise in removing my ornaments? Some of the clasps were, every now and then, tricky even for me and I put on and remove my ornaments all the time. Had he done this many times before with others? Then, returning to my senses, I chastised myself: don't let suspicions ruin the moment, just enjoy it.

Sometimes I would keep my eyes open, wanting to see for myself the intense desire in his, but his eyes would be shut, not tightly, just dreamily half-closed. Once he caught me looking at him and asked with a smile, 'Why do you keep your eyes open my love? Let all your senses be absorbed in this moment of our love-making. If you take away one of your senses, the others will be heightened. So close your eyes, let there be darkness and nothing else.' But when I wanted to share with him the overwhelming emotions I experienced in his company, he always seemed to know what I wanted to say and would put his hand on my mouth and beg me to be silent. The most important things are the hardest to express, he said. 'Words do not always do justice to our thoughts and sensations. If we clothe them ineptly in words, we diminish not only the meaning but also the very feelings we want to convey. Be silent, then, and let them reside in you for ever.' And I would shut my eyes and shudder at the strange sensation of imploding with all the happiness running amok in me.

There were days when Shiva's adoring eyes watched my every move, even while I lined my fish-shaped eyes with kohl or combed out the tangles in my long hair after a night of passion. In the same way, Shiva's every movement, every mood, every expression held me in thrall. When he danced, lost in the cosmic beat of the music within him, celebrating the destruction of some demon or the other, I sat gazing in wonder, the tinkling of the kinkinis on his feet reverberating in my ears. Sometimes I would join him and we would dance together, and even compete with each other to create new rhythms and movements.

As with all couples, however, it was not always smooth and peaceful between us. We were often impatient with each other and exchanged harsh words. Once, while quarrelling over a trivial matter, Shiva said that my mind was mired in turbidness like the mass of clouds on the peak of the Himalaya, and my heart was unfathomable because I had inherited hardness from the mountain rocks, impenetrability from its forests and crookedness from its rivers. I was hurt and furious, but as always I did not hesitate to speak my mind and retaliated, saying, 'From those serpents that coil around your neck you have received many tongues, the ashes you rub on your body have made you secretive and surreptitious, and the wickedness of your heart has sprung from the blemished moon that nestles in your hair. '

I knew Shiva was sometimes unwittingly harsher than the occasion demanded, but I often found his teasing too much to bear. One night, while we lay next to each other, exhausted from our passions, he began gloating over his 'fairer' skin, conveniently disregarding the fact that he attained this hue only due to the ashes he smeared all over himself! He tossed his arm around my neck and said in an indolent tone, 'Look, your slender body joined with mine shines darkly upon my white body. It looks like a black serpent coiled around a white sandalwood tree; you are like the night touched by the light of the dark side of the moon—indeed, you offend my sight.' I recoiled at this slight and instantly released myself from his embrace. 'I sought to win your heart with shining acts of asceticism and my reward for it is dishonour?' I lashed out. 'I am hardly the black one for are *you* not known to all as Mahakala? I am not crooked like a snake; you are the one who possesses poison.' A look of surprise and hurt shaded Shiva's face, and he said, 'I did not mean to blame you, it was with the intention of flattering you that I spoke in jest. You have a mind as clear as a rock crystal, but people like us whose dark bodies are smeared with white ashes have one thought in the heart while our words express the opposite. If you are angry at this I will not speak to you in jest again, O terrifying goddess. Control your wrath. I bow before you and fold my hands in reverence.' Shiva's eyes mirrored his concern and contrition and I succumbed to his soothing words. He had a compelling power over me; a simple smile from him could lift my spirits and rid my mind of all negative emotions.

However, it was not often that I got the luxury to contemplate my lord and revel in his being. For Shiva, the beloved of so many, the devotee of his devotees, was constantly surrounded by an entourage of his ganas, led by Narada, Bhringi and the ever-faithful Nandi. For instance, playing chausara, the dice game (though one of my favourite pastimes because it gave me the chance to match wits with Shiva) always turned out to be a trying experience for me. Whenever we played, Shiva's cronies would crowd around us to cheer their lord. I would have put up with it all, of course, if I was not targeted as Shiva's rival by them. Whenever it was my turn they would burst into some silly love song or lament tunelessly so that I would get distracted and Shiva could win. In fact, their behaviour would become all the more childish and fatuous when I started to win, and if indeed I did, my victory was invariably attributed to my skills at cheating, not to my intelligence or my ability to anticipate Shiva's moves. Such situations would leave me muttering under my breath, while Shiva smiled indulgently at his crew and even dared to laugh at my growing irritation.

On one such occasion, I got my own back. We had played for almost half the afternoon, when Shiva began to lose. When the dice came to me, I rolled the cubes between my palms for a long time, pretending to concentrate like never before, fully aware that the sweet tinkling of my glass bangles would drive Shiva and his minions quite crazy. I could feel Shiva's eyes watching me; no doubt he was wondering what was taking me so long, but he did not betray his impatience. Finally, I let the dice fall, and I won! Almost instantly Shiva's allies started accusing me of winning by unfair means. 'Don't you think it is a little too obvious how impartial you all are towards your lord?' I retorted, emboldened by my victory in the game. Then I addressed Shiva. 'Remove the moon that adorns your hair, for it now belongs to me.' I had expected a scowl and a gruff refusal but, to my utmost surprise, he meekly complied. Triumphant at possessing the lovely glowing moon, I wore it as an earring. Then I said, 'Hand me all your ornaments.' To my amazement he acquiesced without a murmur to this as well, though I could feel the disapproving eyes of Narada and his friends on me. Finally I said, 'Now take off your loin cloth, my lord.' A collective gasp of disbelief broke the sullen silence around us and Shiva snapped angrily, 'What?' I had been expecting an outburst, and I smiled sweetly and said, 'What have you to do with a loin cloth, O Shiva? Are you not a sanctified soul? Sometime back you wandered in the Daruvana forest with nothing on you.' I had been waiting for a chance to chastise him about that indiscretion, and now I had done it with a smile on my face! But as I watched hurt and bewilderment

132

cloud his otherwise tranquil face, I grew contrite for taking advantage of his simplicity and his love for me. Shiva is truly Bholanath—as his devotees refer to him— so pure at heart and so unworldly; but with who else can I take such liberties?

It is true that I have nothing but admiration for the tremendous devotion that Shiva inspires in his followers, but I often find their behaviour tiresome, to say the least. They are wary of Rudra's anger yet their love for him frequently borders on obsession.

It once happened that Shiva and I were blessing a group of sages and ordinary folk who had gathered to pay homage to us. They circumambulated us and sought our blessings by touching their foreheads to our feet. It was a particularly hot summer afternoon and I stood there silently, shifting my weight from one foot to the other, a little tired but happy to be surrounded by our devotees. The pugnacious Bhringi was present in the gathering and when his turn came to seek our blessings, Maheshwara's dogged follower bowed his head before Shiva and circumambulated him alone, ignoring me completely, as though worshipping me would make him impure in some way. A gasp of surprise rose in the hall and I was furious at such a demeaning slur. I looked at Shiva, who stood awkwardly, embarrassment written all over his face, but instead of admonishing Bhringi, Mahadeva showered him with blessings just as he had on those who had come before. Silently I made up my mind that some day I would assume such a form that neither Bhringi nor any other ardent devotee of Shiva would ever ignore me again.

Thousands of years later, when Shiva and I appeared to our devotees in the conjoined form of Ardhanarishwara, I was complacent that my wish to get the better of Bhringi would now come true. I now constituted Shiva's left half while he made up my right. Bhringi, I was certain, would not be able to offend me again. When he saw the two of us one-bodied, Bhringi's facial expression belied any disappointment he may have felt at not being able to pay obeisance to his chosen deity. I waited for him to start circumambulating us, but to my astonishment the audacious sage strode off without bowing even to his lord! Shiva looked startled but it was not in his nature to comment on such matters, and so he kept quiet.

But, ah, the divine should never underestimate the bhakti of the dedicated follower. After years of performing rigorous tapas, Bhringi was granted his desire to begin another life in the form of a beetle. It was in this form that he once again approached our Ardhanarishwara composite. Slowly and skilfully he pierced a hole between the two of us and simply circumambulated Shiva's side of our joint body! I could not help but admire Bhringi's steadfast faithfulness to his lord, and I praised Shiva yet again for his unmatched ability to arouse such fervent loyalty.

There was one, however, whose proximity to Shiva I found difficult to tolerate. This was Ganga, the source of the waters that flow from Shiva's jata and purify the earth. In all the years of my being Shiva's consort, I had been acutely uneasy with her perennial presence on my husband's head. Shiva and I argued endlessly about her. Of scourse, Shiva had a rational explanation for her constant presence, and I too know how he had to step in to trap Ganga's unruly waters in his jata to save humanity from certain extinction. But the way she flowed through Shiva's locks, first in little gurgling streams, then rollicking and gushing joyously, almost seductively, down his face, drove me berserk with envy.

Ganga was witness to everything Shiva did. She was with him even when he retired to remote mountain peaks to do tapas and could not be approached by anyone. She was present during our embraces, our quarrels, our hours spent with the worshippers. And she didn't look the least bit 'trapped', mind you. In fact, she showed no signs of consternation, fear or guilt. If you ask me, she seemed quite happy up there, caressing Shiva, breathing in tune with him. Did she even want to find a way out of her hair-snare, I wondered. Sometimes I could feel Ganga's eyes taunting me, as though the pleasure she experienced in Shiva's proximity was greater than my own. The thought gnawed at me till I thought I was going insane.

As always, Shiva knew just how to placate me. When I told him of my agitation, he wrapped his arms around me, smothering my protests as my mouth was muffled by his chest, and said, 'I have never seen you look so beautiful.' And as our bodies united for the umpteenth time, I quite forgot that he had other distractions too—the world to take care of, brash rivers to be tamed, wicked demons to be destroyed, clever sages to be rewarded, devout devotees to be blessed with his lofty grace.

So many times I have watched my Chandrashekhara, the moon-crested one, as he sat motionless in meditation under a banyan tree, the adi yogi. His hair, long, tangled and matted, spreading over his broad shoulders; his face gleaming with the moon's soft glow; his eyes seeing but never really watching, oblivious to the surroundings, awake only to the soul within, his ash-besmeared chest adorned with glistening serpents entwined with each other as if they did not ever want to let go. In the calmness that emanated from his being, the insects and birds fell silent and even the air stilled. He seemed to be surrounded by a luminous aura, resulting from his lofty wisdom, his constant immersion in tapas and the effortless suppression of his innate passions.

Yet Shiva's remarkable stillness often aroused in me feelings of insecurity and loneliness, especially when he retreated to the mountains for many years at a time. When I told him of my fears, he said, 'Why are you afraid of being alone, O goddess? I would understand your trepidation if there was a second entity in the universe, but there is none. I am Brahman, I am everything, I represent advaita. The illusion of dvaita, O goddess, results from avidya. What delusion and what grief can there be for one who knows the truth: I reside in everything, even in you.'

For a while I found comfort in this profound thought. But I could not dismiss the sense of isolation that sometimes overwhelmed me and I started yearning for the love and protection of a son. Besides, it was my duty to remind Shiva of his responsibility to protect the universe. The gods, after all, had arranged our union for a purpose. Taraka, the demon, was still terrorizing them and they needed our offspring to arrive soon. I knew this would not happen if Shiva was unwilling, for offspring were not the natural result of our love-making—being a Mahayogi, Shiva preferred to retain his seed rather than to shed it.

Knowing how dismissive Shiva was about earthly bonds, I rehearsed what seemed like a convincing argument that could change his mind. When he returned home from a long sojourn in the mountains, I broached the subject and said, 'What about your three rinas, the debts you owe, to the rishis, to the gods, and to the ancestors by begetting sons who will make the funereal offerings?' To my utmost chagrin, Shiva had his reply ready, 'There are three worlds: the world of ancestors, the world of the sages and the world of the gods. Of these, the world of the ancestors is to be attained through a son and by no other rite or meditation; the world of the sages through the agnihotra homa—neither through the son nor through meditation; and the world of gods only through meditation. The last is the best of the three worlds, and meditation is the true path.' Then he added, 'For the householder, the son is a source of comfort and enjoyment to his father and in death the son performs rituals to grant his dead father safe passage into better rebirths. I am Shiva and as Shiva I have no death and hence no need for such rites. Where there is no disease where is the need for a cure? I desire to be detached and free, not for me a son. Let us rejoice in the pleasures between man and woman without thinking about our progeny.'

Exasperated, I decided to take matters into my own hands and arouse Shiva's passion as never before, but that too was fraught with obstacles, what with the gods, anxious for the birth of our son, constantly interrupting our love-making. First the insecure and selfish Indra complained to Brahma, 'O Creator, all the worlds have been agitated by the coition of Hara with Parvati. I myself have been greatly terrified and have come to take refuge in you. If this coition goes on uninterrupted, I fear that the son that will be born out of the sexual intercourse will overpower me! Do take such steps so that his son shall not oppress me and the other gods: save us from that great impending danger.' Saying this, he landed up outside our chambers to reassert his position among the gods. Another time, the whole horde had the audacity to interrupt us because, they claimed, the intensity of our love-making was disturbing the universe! 'The earth trembles and none of the gods can find any peace,' they said, addressing Shiva. 'Take pity on us all. Abandon your mahamaithuna and indulge in mere love-play.'

Then, as though they hadn't caused enough trouble already, they suddenly grew perturbed by the delay in the birth of our offspring, and wondered, 'Why does Shiva delay? He married for us. Why is he procrastinating?' Agni and a few others arrived at Kailash to check on us. Nandi, faithful as ever, tried to stop them from entering our chambers, and in the confusion that ensued, Agni managed to slip in, even as Shiva was in the acme of bliss. Suddenly aware of unwanted company, Shiva looked around and as I looked away in embarrassment Shiva's seed spurted out. Since the gods had caused this misfortune, they now carried Shiva's seed in turn till finally they deposited it in the care of the Krittikas, the six forest virgins—and Skanda, my son, was born.

Thus, through much trial, tribulation and heartache did I become a mother to Skanda, my son Karttikeya, who vanquished the demon Taraka in a fierce battle when he was just six days old. My other son, Ganesha, also born under trying circumstances, was the apple of my eye and would grow to be the most widely worshipped deity among mortals. Our offspring had combined in their natures the best of me and the best of Shankara. Their accomplishments filled me with pride.

Together, as a family, we continue to protect the universe, to sustain creation, to nourish life, and by our collective grace and blessings humanity will continue to prosper.

Literally, Parvati means 'of the mountains'. Several epithets attributed to Parvati relate her to mountains—Girija, Shailasuta, Himalayaputri and, the oldest, Haimavati. Significantly, both Parvati and Shiva are associated with mountains. Parvati's parents are the eponymous Himavat and Mena. Some Puranas tell us that the goddess resided in the Vindhyas, a fact emphasized by her epithet Vindhyavasini, the form in which she is worshipped at a place near Mirzapur where the Vindhyas approach the Ganga.[1] In certain myths Shiva and Parvati are said to be living on Mount Mandara, a mythical mountain at times identified with a hill to the south of Bhagalpur in Bihar.[2]

As a land type, mountains have attracted and provided refuge and solace to mystics, ascetics, monks, truth-seekers, hermits and ordinary people alike. Many traditions believe that mountain peaks are the points where heaven and earth meet and where gods reside. Perhaps because of their inaccessibility and the mystery and intrigue shrouding them, mountains are considered holy in many faiths and figure prominently in many religions as sacred venues. Even today scaling the peak of a mountain amounts to a 'conquest' and is seen as a human and spiritual feat. The Himalayan peaks are named after the gods who are believed to have lived there and are considered of prime importance because they are the source of holy rivers.

A Marriage Made in Heaven

The episode of Parvati's severe penance to win over Shiva as a bridegroom is a familiar episode in pan-Indian mythological narratives and is well elaborated in Sanskritic sources as well. The sacred marriage of Shiva and Parvati, referred to as 'kalyanasundaram' or 'Parvati parinaya' when depicted in sculpture, is richly recorded in much textual material, such as the Tamil Talapuranas, which constitute the sacred history of a particular place. The Talapurana of the temple-city of Madurai and its breathtaking Meenakshi Amman temple is an example. Like the other temples in South India, which annually celebrate marriages between gods and goddesses, the Madurai temple celebrates the marriage of Shiva and Parvati as its principal festival. The Talapuranas contain scattered references to Shiva's capacity to be wild, unpredictable, even insulting. He frightens faithless kings, instigates devotees to steal money from the royal treasury and appears in the form of a lazy mud-slinging workman who demands money for work he refuses to perform. Still, he is a model bridegroom for the king's daughter Meenakshi, a common epithet for Parvati in South India. Instead of a carrier of skulls who frequents cremation grounds, here he is Sundareshwara, the beautiful lord.

Parvati's presence beside Shiva accentuates his wholeness as, through their union, he is inducted into worldly life, extending his range of activities to the domestic hearth after being associated with destruction, liminal spaces such as the cremation grounds and followers of grotesque shape and strange behaviour. As Parvati, the goddess brings a semblance of order into Shiva's life, albeit one based on brahmanical principles. Parvati's undertaking is to tempt Shiva away from asceticism, yoga and his other preoccupations. She firmly upholds the dictates of dharma: Next to sacrifice, the obligation to get married and procreate is central to brahmanical theology, which regards only the person who has a family—constituting father, mother and son—as a complete person. In the role of the householder, Parvati emphasizes the significance of life in this world and represents the beauty and attraction of married life, the very values the renouncer has rejected to become an ascetic. Undoubtedly, Shiva and the goddess may be worshipped independently of each other (and she is, as Durga, Kali, and in many other forms), but for those who like to see them as a couple she is a key player in Shaiva mythology and theology.

As Shiva is an ascetic, it is in the gods' interest to find a goddess proficient enough to beguile Shiva into marriage, and who better than Shakti herself, who will spiritedly take up the challenge? Moreover, the gods are well aware that the intensity of Shiva's tapas generates vast quantities of energy which must be used in creative ways, and when passed on to his offspring along with the goddess's ferocious strength their combined energy will create the ultimate weapon against an evil demon.

But their coming together in marriage will clearly not be smooth, for Shiva has a characteristic aversion to worldly ties, particularly of the female kind. In the Shiva Purana the almighty god blatantly declares: 'There is much base bondage in the world. Association with women is the toughest of all. One can free oneself from all bondages except that of women.'[3]

Active engagement through asceticism or tapas is advocated as the cultural prerequisite for union with Shiva. Hence, even in the celestial world, Parvati takes the form of a human disciple, dresses in the clothes of an ascetic, complete with a jata and modest diet, and remains in one-pointed tapas till Shiva accepts her as his wife. Images of Parvati in tapas are seen in profusion in temple art from the seventh century CE, though a few early representations dating back to the second century have been found in Mathura.[4] By insisting on performing tapas, Parvati actively subverts her established mode of behaviour as a woman, or what is termed in the shastras as 'stridharma', thus challenging normative social dictates. The dharmashastras certainly do not prescribe that women should leave home and hearth and retire to the wilderness to perform austerities. As a matter of fact, Parvati's tapas advocates yoga as a higher form of love than sexuality. By communicating the idea that passion has to be controlled, not denied, Parvati becomes the model yogini.[5] The fire of her lust gets transmuted into the fire of asceticism.

Shiva, whose attention she wishes to gain, is the great ascetic, the only god who stays in the state of yoga and bhoga simultaneously. Early sculptures depict an obviously ithyphallic Shiva seated in a yogic posture. Shiva is the ideal yati and the ideal pati and represents a wholesome balance between the polarities of asceticism and eroticism.

Parvati and Shiva are the primordial couple, the exemplary husband-and-wife pair of the Hindu pantheon. They share a far more egalitarian relationship as compared to other coupled deities.

Quarrels are an important part of the mythology of Shiva and Parvati. They demonstrate the conflict between the divergent aspects that Shiva represents. Again, the quarrels may be looked upon as a sign of cultic conflict between two powerful deities who have perforce been brought together through marriage. Moreover, quarrels, separation, placating and eventual harmony are essential ingredients of any sexual relationship. The passion aroused by the tumult is usually looked upon as an intensifying element spurring the erotic mood.

Many erstwhile powerful goddesses were turned into utterly subservient wives in accordance with the conception of proper connubial conduct in a patriarchal society and were offered as models for emulation by mortal women. However, the codes of feminine conduct laid down in the shastras were not always reflected or translated in myth or art. It is a hallmark of Shaiva mythology that Parvati is allowed autonomy in her different forms and is far more spirited as a wife than several other goddesses. In fact, while daughters in Indian households are often compared to Lakshmi or Sita, rarely do we hear of a girl being likened to Parvati or being told to emulate her in any way.

The spirited exchanges between Shiva and Parvati indicate to us not only the goddess's power to hold her own in her relationship with Shiva, as she does in every other sphere, but also Shiva's greatness as he deals with this power in charming and very human ways. The varying versions of the story of Shiva teasing Parvati about her complexion show her reacting differently to the situation. In our narrative she asserts herself and refuses to give in and change her natural, perhaps dusky, colouring. Here is an instance of the more common response. According to the Skanda Purana, Parvati tells Shiva, 'If you are displeased with my colour, how is it that you have made love to me for so long? There is nothing in the universe that is unachievable for my lord, the lord of the universe. Though she may possess all other qualities, the life of a woman is in vain if her husband does not delight in her. Hence, eschewing this colour censured by you, I shall attain another colour, or I shall cease to exist myself.' Bent upon penance, she requests for permission from her lord to leave his company. 'As I rose from the bed, my heart weary that I would have to leave my household, Shiva replied, "Why are you angry with me, not recognizing this as a jocular remark of mine? If I am not delighted with you, where else can I seek delight? You are the mother of this universe and I am its father and lord."'[6]

It is believed even today that when Shiva is angry he may wreak havoc on the world, but when appeased and calm he is a model husband. Young girls from different parts of the country are taught to worship the Shiva linga with water and milk to cool his anger, observe fasts and dedicate themselves to his service in order to win a husband who meets Shiva's ideal. This has somewhat surprised many, for the question that is raised is whether he was really such an 'ideal husband' on all counts.

Shiva is loath to have children, he is perpetually absorbed in otherworldly affairs, his attire (or the lack of it), his habitat, his companions—all go against the grain, so to speak. Nevertheless in his life there is place for a spouse who is his equal on all counts and who is clearly important to him. Shiva and Parvati complement each other, more than any other celestial couple, and their skirmishes with each other show in high relief the foibles each possesses.

The Other Woman

By the beginning of the Christian era the rivers Ganga and Yamuna, along with a host of other rivers, were personified and invoked as deities as their waters were considered sacred. Ganga, the supremely revered river, is often described as Shiva's second love in iconography and mythology. In Bengali oral tradition, Ganga is identified as Shiva's first wife. As for Shiva, a well-known epithet attributed to him is 'Gangadhara', or 'the one who carries Ganga', since Ganga flows to earth from his jata.

The myth involving Shiva and Ganga tells us that after practising austerities for many years, the mortal Bhagiratha obtained Ganga's consent to descend to earth to wash away the ashes of the sixty thousand sons of Sagara and free their spirits. But in order to save the earth from the danger of being swept away by the impact of the heavenly waters, Bhagiratha requested Shiva to receive the celestial river and then release her to the earth, and Shiva readily agreed. Ganga, however, voiced her doubts about Shiva's efficacy in the situation. Convinced that not even Mahadeva was strong enough to withstand her might, the mischievous maiden decided to use the force of her descent to push Shiva down to the netherworld. But Shiva caught her in the tangles of his locks and kept her bound there for several thousand years. The myth is significant because it connects Shiva to a cosmogonic act which brings celestial, life-giving waters to the human world.

In many art forms Ganga is shown either as a minuscule woman perched on top of Shiva's matted locks, or as a river streaming down from his topknot. Shiva's countenance, meanwhile, bears a tranquil expression as though he is oblivious of her presence and proximity. Ganga was no doubt beneficial to the world, and Shiva helped in his own way to prevent a calamity from befalling the earth. However, in charmingly human interpretations of the myth, Parvati sees their association as a secret love affair. Through complaints and in colourful dialogue with Shiva, Parvati displays and expresses the jealousy of a long-suffering and insecure wife. Having said this, mention must be made of a particular inscription in which Ganga is portrayed as being jealous of the closeness Parvati shares with Shiva in the Ardhanarishwara form: 'May the divine Ganga on Shiva's head protect you, she who is attenuated as it were with jealousy at seeing half his body appropriated by the daughter of the mountains.'[7]

In a sculpture depicting the Gangadharamurti image of Shiva at the Gangaikonda Cholapuram temple, Maheshwara, with four hands, is depicted as releasing the pent-up Ganga from his matted locks by stretching a coil of hair with one of his right hands, while he caresses his principle consort Parvati with the other right hand as if to pacify her jealousy towards her co-wife. Interestingly, Parvati has her revenge in a verse of the *Saundaryalahari* (c. eighth or ninth century CE), controversially attributed to Shankaracharya, which extols the grace and benevolence of the goddess. The verse describes Shiva prostrating before her, and Ganga, who sits customarily on Shiva's head, has to flow over Parvati's feet, thereby showing her respect for Shiva's consort in a ritual laving of the deity's feet.[8]

Ardhanarishwara

The Ardhanarishwara image—in which the left half of Shiva's body is female, with all the physical and ornamental accoutrements, and the right has the male features of Shiva—represents the fusion of Shiva with Parvati.

This iconographic-mythological image has long been subjected to perplexing interpretations, and disciples, via poetry or legend, have tried to comprehend it in their own ways, sometimes evoking humour. Folklore has it that the fusion took place because Parvati wanted to keep an eye on Shiva and stymie his philandering—which was always a possibility with the nubile Ganga seated right on his head! A certain verse mentions Shiva's delight in receiving Parvati's tight embrace in this form, but comments that his heart must often grieve because he cannot look into her eyes any more.

On a philosophical plane the Ardhanarishwara is a creative union of the active and the passive principles of creation, the male representing the passive purusha (Shiva) and the female the active prakriti (Shakti). It is the fusion of the formless wholeness of Brahman with the creative energy of existence, Parvati. Shiva and Shakti thus share the ultimate dialectical relationship and are incomplete without each other. It is only through Shakti, now inherent in him, that Shiva realizes his true nature. The image indicates that Shiva is actually both the eternal male and the eternal female. As half- male and half-female he visibly reconciles the polarities of existence in his own being.

The idea of wholesome and holistic harmony between the male and female aspects of creative energy is reflected in the physical representation of the image as well. In the figure of the Ardhanarishwara there seems to be an interchangeability and a flow between the male and female forms rather than a sharp demarcation between the two. Not only are Shiva and Parvati unmistakably shown to be the primordial pair, but the image also ensures that Shiva is no longer assigned a merely negative stature with the specific task of destruction, as was the case in the earliest depictions. However, since Shiva and Parvati have been fused into a single form, the Ardhanarishwara prevents sexual union. They must separate from each other in order to have sexual intercourse.

In some instances the image has been used to promote the notion of women's equality. However, it is necessary to study the specific ways in which the male and female aspects have been constructed and defined in Indian tradition to see if in fact the image is a positive, emancipatory ideal for women, and for men for that matter.[9] While the male and female halves of the image are of equal physical stature, the name given to the icon—Ardhanarishwara—does not translate as 'half-woman, half-man', but rather as 'lord who is half-woman'. The epithet thus represents a masculine concept which incorporates a female partnership—Shiva's generative force, when he assumes the role of creator, requires a female presence. This immediately suggests a gender hierarchy because the male half of the icon is given the privileged title 'Ishwara' which means god, lord, master, whereas the female half is simply designated as 'nari', woman. The name, then, does not convey equal status for both halves.

The icon may also be seen as a symbol of the syncretic ideology. Syncretism represents a blending of distinct or even opposite cultures to form an apparent or quasi-new entity or subculture. The Ardhanarishwara may thus signify the coming together of two sects in one form to allay sectarian tendencies lurking in the minds of the followers. With more or less equal status in the Ardhanarishwara form, both Shiva and Parvati would, willy-nilly, have to be simultaneously worshipped. Whether exclusive tendencies of sectarianism were finally overcome with this composite form is a matter of debate and a conclusion may only be arrived at through micro-regional studies. The myth involving Bhringi and Ardhanarishwara, where Bhringi devices a unique strategy to worship the deity of his choice by persistently separating the rather composite pair, may just as well indicate the non-acceptance of syncretism.

On yet another level the image is a pointer to the bisexual creative principle where the godhead transcends sexual particularity, or, more accurately, includes both dimensions, that is, male and female, father and mother, which leads to the hybridization of the form. The yoking together of the two is a sign of having successfully coped with or transcended one's deepest conflicts about femininity and masculinity. Whatever it be, one who is close to godliness is expected to show less concern with the worldly division between genders; the important thing is to possess the ability to transcend the barriers imposed by one's sexual selfhood, and thereby reflect the values which are unfettered by society's prevalent sexual identities.

Ultimately, the message the image delivers is one of advaita. The fusion of the masculine and feminine in the androgynous form is a partial attainment en route to transcendence where all forms ultimately collapse and erode in the mystery and fluidity of organic singularity, that is, advaita.

The Challenge of Reconciliation

Eventually, Shiva marries Parvati, but in his reluctance to produce offspring he perpetuates the tension between the ascetic ideal and the householder ideal. The philosophical tussle between pravritti and nivritti, which buoyantly appears in most of the important Shiva myths has been referred to in previous chapters. Shiva, in fact, appears to be the repository of this early leitmotif of Hindu thought.

A somewhat parallel situation is to be found in a particularly well-known story in the oldest of the Upanishads, the Brihadaranyaka Upanishad, which dates back to the eighth century BC, a period that is historically concomitant with the disintegration of old Vedic values.

The rishi Yajnavalkya, ready to shift to a different mode of living, decides to renounce his life as a householder and take up the sanyas ashrama. As he is about to divide his property between his two wives Maitreyi and Katyayani, Maitreyi, who does not have a son from Yajnavalkya (from Katyayani he has three), asks him, 'If I were to possess this whole world filled with riches, would it make me immortal?' Yajnavalkya replies that immortality cannot be attained through wealth or through rites performed with wealth. So Maitreyi asks him, 'What shall I do with that which will not make me immortal?' Yajnavalkya requests her to take a seat and explains to her the meaning of the Self with a view to teaching renunciation as a means to immortality. He tells her that the Self is dearer than a son, therefore our love for other objects is secondary since they contribute to the pleasure of the Self, while our love for the Self is primary and should be realized.

In Indian tradition the family line is said to continue through the son despite the death of the father. As the son survives after the father's death, so the father survives his own death through his son and the family is guaranteed immortality. By not fulfilling this aspect of Vedic culture with Maitreyi, Yajnavalkya deprives her of a chance at immortality. The belief that the father continues to exist in his son finds ritual expression in the ceremony of transmission (sampratti or sampradana) which is performed when the father's death is imminent. According to the Kaushitaki Upanishad, the son lies on top of the father touching each of his father's limbs with his own. The father then delivers all his faculties to the son and the son accepts them. As he departs, the father enters the son and through him stands firm in the world.

The mythology of Shiva brings to a conscious level the fundamental cultural quandary of choosing between living in the social world, which includes certain commitments and the performance of familial duty and enjoyment of sensual pleasure, and the path of renunciation, which rejects the world and denies sexuality and procreation in order to attain spiritual salvation. This issue, though persistently confronted in Shaiva mythology, is never fully resolved. In the myths the constant toss up for Shiva is between being the solitary one, as depicted in the early texts where he is Rudra, and becoming a householder and begetting sons. However, the conflict between two contrary modes of life does yield to a vision of reconciliation, interdependence and symbiotic harmony which can be seen in the different manifestations of the linga–yoni, Ardhanarishwara, Shiva–Shakti, Gauri–Shankara, Uma–Maheshwara.

It must be remembered, however, that both Shiva and the goddess individually engage in mythologically meaningful acts, such as Durga's slaying of Mahishasura, or Shiva's beheading of Ganesha, who is his son by virtue of being created by Parvati. These acts emphasize the power and efficacy of the individual divinities and recall, with some measure of nostalgia, their past aloneness before they were 'householded'.

❧❦ Ganesha ❧❦

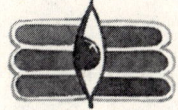

I am Ganesha. They call me Ganapati, lord of the people.

By the blessings of my illustrious parents—Shiva
and Parvati—I am the deity most frequently worshipped
by mortals and immortals. The mighty, the weak,
everyone bows to me before embarking on a personal
mission, however significant or mundane it may be,
for I possess the power to plant and remove hurdles
and hindrances in the path of prosperity and well-being.
Anxious students invoke my blessings before examinations,
thrifty traders and prudent merchants pray to me on the
eve of critical transactions, itinerant travellers bow before
me prior to a journey of adventure. Why, even Shiva
himself ran into trouble because he forgot to pray to me
before his battle against the demon rulers of Tripura! I
may not possess my father's cosmic wholeness or my
mother's fierce grace, but my reputation as the wise,

accessible, munificent Vijneshwara, the remover of obstacles, has made me more popular than any of the other gods.

My unusual appearance has earned me many affectionate names from my devotees. I am the elephant-headed Gajanana; I am Ekadanta, proud bearer of a single tusk; I am Vakratunda, with a twisted elephant's trunk for a nose; I am Lambodara, the pot-bellied one. I was not born with an elephant's head, however. My mother had lovingly shaped me with her own hands into a charming little boy; the elephant's head was my father Shankara's contribution, from my first, rather unfortunate, encounter with him.

In fact, each time I asked my mother about my birth she would tell me a different story. When I was very young I would be flattered that she thought of so many variations to amuse me, but as I grew older the sheer variety of the stories left me musing about my arrival in the world. It also bothered me a great deal to know that my father did not want a child at all, to begin with, and had nothing to do with my birth. But now that I am aware of Shiva's ways, it all makes sense and I feel blessed to be so closely associated with him.

Whichever story I got to hear, it always made me feel special to know how much my mother wanted me in her life. My mother, Parvati, had for a long time wished for a son of her own who would be loyal and loving to her and whom she could fuss over and depend on while

Shiva was away on his long sojourns into the forests and mountains for uninterrupted tapas. But being averse to worldly relations and attachments Shiva never complied with her desire. They argued incessantly over this until Parvati found the perfect opportunity to create a child without Shiva's involvement.

It so happened that one day Parvati's friends Jaya and Vijaya complained to her that they could not enjoy any privacy in their chambers since all the gatekeepers owed their allegiance to Lord Shiva and the women had no control over them. 'They allow anyone to come into our residences at the most awkward times and the most untimely intruder is often your spouse, Shiva,' they told her. 'He does not realize his transgression because he is Mahakala himself, and he walks through our chambers at any hour, without a care for our convenience, while we dart about hither and thither. Why cannot we have our own gatekeeper to watch our rooms?' Parvati too had been thinking about this for a while. She herself was quite fed up with Shiva's unannounced intrusions into her private chambers, especially when she was enjoying a quiet moment of leisure in her bath. But where were they to find a loyal, trustworthy soul who would answer to Parvati alone?

Parvati came up with the perfect plan to solve the problem, one that would give her the satisfaction of becoming a mother as well. After all, a son she created on her own would not owe allegiance to anybody else and she could place her trust unquestioningly in him. She made a paste of scented unguents and powder and spread it over her body with slow strokes. The palms of her hands rubbed over her stomach, her legs, her breasts, mixing the lepa with her sweat and flakes of spent skin. When she was satisfied, she gathered the mixture together in a lump, lovingly fashioned a little boy out of it and gave it life. That was me. Since I was created when Parvati was 'vina nayakana', that is, in the absence of her husband, I am popularly known as Vinayaka.

From the time I was born I hardly ever left my mother's side. With nothing to distract her from me and no Shiva to bond with, Parvati showered me with love and attention. Often she would tell me tales about my father, about his encounters with Andhaka or Kamadeva and how he had saved creation many times from being destroyed. Listening to her, I would wonder at Shiva's splendid resolve and power and long for the day we would meet. Little did I know how fateful that meeting was to be.

Most infants have no recollection of the first time their eyes meet their father's, or for that matter, even their mother's. But my first meeting with my father is sharply etched in my mind. It was as violent and regrettable as, I imagine, my introduction to my mother was gentle and comforting. Endless kathas describing the incident and recited and recounted by innumerable priests and devotees will never let me forget it.

One day Parvati sat me down and told me, 'I am stationing you here at the threshold of my bath chamber, my son. Guard it well. Nobody should enter till I am done. It is a position of great responsibility and I trust you will be vigilant and not let me down.'

I was flattered by her trust in me and stood at the door with my hands on my hips, ready to take on anybody who approached Parvati's chamber. While instructing me to guard the door and keep intruders out, Parvati had not mentioned any person for whom I was to make an exception. She should, perhaps, have told me about the tall man with matted locks, who might come seeking her company, bearing a trident in one hand, with a brilliant aura emanating from his person—Shiva, my father. But, alas, my knowledge was incomplete and I was not discerning enough to know whom to keep out and whom to permit. So when a stranger wearing an animal skin and covered in ashes strode purposefully up to the door, more than eager to make an entrance, I stood in his way. Bursting with self-importance and pride, and eager to fulfil the first serious task my mother had allotted me, I did not flinch.

At first the man looked at me in amusement, but when he took a step forward and I firmly blocked his way, his indulgent smile quickly disappeared and he looked mildly annoyed. Without raising his voice, he commanded, 'Move out of my way, young one.' When I did not budge and sternly announced that I would not give way, his eyes blazed with anger, 'Do you know who I am?' he thundered. 'I am Shiva, Parvati's spouse, the lord of the universe. I have free access to the entire cosmos, let alone my wife's chamber. Who are you to stop me?' Still blocking the passage, I retorted just as tartly, 'Never mind who I am. I have never seen you before. Parvati is taking a bath and you cannot go inside.'

It is true that Shiva revealed his identity to me but my task was clear to me and my mother was depending on me to fulfil it. Besides, how was I to be sure he was who he claimed to be? I had never set eyes on him before. Not knowing that I was Parvati's son, and therefore his own, Shiva lost his temper and instructed his followers to remove me from my station. When I single-handedly defeated all of them, Shiva, by now infuriated with me, raised his trishul. A sharp pain shot through my neck before darkness descended over my eyes.

Hearing the commotion outside, Parvati rushed out of her bath. She later told me that seeing me, her beloved son, lying headless on the ground, she was overwrought with grief and disbelief at what Shiva had done. But steadily her grief transformed into fury. Shiva tried to placate her, pleading innocence since he had had no idea of my identity, but she would not be calmed. She told him that unless he restored my life she would take the form of Kali and bring the universe to destruction. Shiva knew that this was no empty threat, and immediately sent off his servants and all the gods, who had gathered to witness the melee, with an instruction to bring back the head of the first living creature they saw. Everyone set off, through forests and over mountains, on foot, or on their mounts or gilded chariots, intent on finding a living creature whose head could replace mine. Vishnu, flying his mount Garuda over a forest in the north, was the first to spot an elephant king asleep on the bank of a river. He cut off the elephant's head with his chakra and returned to Kailash, where Shiva placed the elephant head on my vacant shoulders and breathed life into me.

When I regained consciousness I found the entire celestial world and Shiva's retinue staring at me, their faces ashen, while my mother sat next to me caressing my limbs. Shiva then approached me, looking apologetic. Still trying to make sense of all that had happened, I looked at him properly for the first time. There was something strangely tranquil about his face that instantly softened my heart and gave me the strength to sit up. Quite forgetting the ordeal I had just been through, I began thinking of all the stories Parvati had told me about Shiva's exploits. I could see before my eyes Mahadeva swallowing the terrible kalakuta, chopping off Brahma's fifth head, setting Kama alight with the rays from his third eye. But now Shiva helped me to my feet and pronounced me Ganapati, the leader of his ganas and made a solemn pledge to my mother that I, her elephant-headed son, would be worshipped before any other god on every auspicious occasion. To celebrate my new life, each god granted me a blessing: Vishnu gave me knowledge, Brahma fame and worship. From Dharma I received righteousness and mercy; from Shiva generosity, peace and self-control; and from Saraswati the powers of speech, poetry, memory and eloquence.

I was happy to be by my mother's side again and delighted at finally having my father around. A while later, my brother Skanda-Karttikeya too returned from one of his many adventures, and we became a complete family. My mother fussed over us a great deal—especially over me, since I was her favourite—while my father sat deep in contemplation. Sometimes Shiva surprised me by placing me on his lap, almost absent-mindedly. There, sitting snugly, I ventured to play with the snakes coiled around his neck. The snakes were slithery and slimy to touch, but afterwards when I wiped my hands together, my palms would feel absolutely dry! In my attempt to nuzzle close to my father, always a little intimidated for he seemed so distant all the time, I would unknowingly rub off some of the ash from his chest and face and try in vain to dust it off me before my mother gave me a round scolding. On a rare occasion, Skanda, who otherwise spent his time practising war moves with his spear and mace, would offer to hold one end of the garland of akanda flowers Parvati was stringing for Shiva to wear, possibly trying to curry favour with her because he knew very well that I was Heramba, Amba's favourite child. What did he expect? Did she not nearly lose me in that calamitous fracas I had with my father? Nandi, the white bull my father rode, usually squatted nearby, gazing placidly into the void, happy just to be by Shiva's side. Nandi was Shiva's eternal companion and his greatest bhakta, and had attained divine wisdom by mere association with Maheshwara. Shiva, too, in his own quiet way, depended very much on Nandi's good sense and absolute loyalty. I watched their closeness with unease, and a little envy, because although we spent much time together as a family, Shiva seemed to remain aloof from me.

Now, I was also Ganapati, leader of Shiva's entourage of quirky, misshapen beings—just like me. At the outset I had grave misgivings about the position granted to me and remained diffident and unsure. I always felt that as the god of war and having displayed his prowess in many battles, Skanda may have nurtured dreams of leading Shiva's ganas. Moreover, it sometimes seemed to me that I had been made Ganapati under duress, as a part of Shiva's attempts to placate my distraught mother while I lay smitten by Shiva's trishul. But I soon decided that I was not going to doubt myself or dwell on past matters; I would deal with situations as they presented themselves to me. Had I not displayed my fighting skills against one as powerful as Shiva, had I not shown my steadfastness to my mother's command? Once I felt more confident about myself I began to relish my new role. In fact, I truly felt I had been born again, as though I had sacrificed my old self to the great Mahadeva and was now doubly blessed.

Through all this I wanted very much to be appreciated by my father, the greatest of all gods. I yearned for his attention and words of approval. I remember hovering around the inner chambers waiting for an opportunity to spend some time with him. One of the things that fascinated me was the ananda tandava, the dance of bliss, which he rendered so wonderfully. With each graceful movement of his limbs, he controlled the very rhythm of the universe. Srishti and pralaya were mere expressions of his dance. I nurtured the desire to imitate this dance of peace and tranquility, of the beatitude of creation. Parvati often joined him in his dance, keeping pace with his rhythm or just clapping to the beat when she got a little tired, and I watched my parents as they moved in tandem. My mother's presence encouraged me and I joined them from time to time, wanting as much to share their joy as to participate in an activity that would catch Shiva's eye. Shiva watched me with some attention but no matter how much I tried to be light-footed and elegant in my movements, he always looked on with an indulgent smile, which made me feel foolish rather than genuinely cherished. Perhaps my large unwieldy body was comical and my movements awkward, I agonized desperately. But such feelings of insecurity vanished when I realized Shiva's true nature.

Once, Shiva sat me down to explain the importance of meditation. 'It is imperative to search for the ultimate truth,' he said.

'What is that?' I asked.

'You will find it if you look inwards. There is so much around us to distort and falsify our understanding of the world. We are misguided into believing that our perception constitutes reality.'

'But I am aware of things around me. Isn't that real?' I said.

'Yes, but it is only representational perception. It is mediated through the senses and sensorial knowledge is imperfect. But there is something beyond the senses, a non-sensory source of knowledge. For example, in the dark you may mistake a rope for a snake . . . If one goes deep there is another reality, the ultimate aspiration of every soul. It is born of intuition; it is what liberates the mind from bondage, the pasha, or noose, created by the senses, which results from avidya.'

But such lofty thoughts did not appeal to me, for I had far to go before I fully comprehended his words. Layer upon layer of conditioning would have to be unveiled for me to attain true understanding.

Then an incident occurred that changed the way I thought about my father and, for that matter, about the universe. Skanda and I had just reached marriageable age and had approached our parents with a request to find brides for us. 'First me,' said I. Skanda, ever ready to whine, said, 'No! It is I who has toiled hard at battles against demons such as Taraka and deserve a comely wife first.' To resolve the prickly situation, our parents presented us with a proposition. There was to be a competition between Skanda and me: we were to race each other around the world and the victorious one would be the first to be blessed with a bride.

Hearing this, Karttikeya mounted his vahana, a rather swift and perky peacock, and rushed off in a hurry. I looked warily at my own vahana, the tiny mushika, and he looked back at me in equal despair. He knew as well as I did that I could never compete with Karttikeya's swiftness. Besides, it came to mind that it would take a rather long time to circle the universe, even for us gods, and I really did not want to be away from my parents for that long. That's when I realized there was no reason for me to despair at my lack of speed, or compete with my brother over trivial issues. All I needed in the universe was right there before me.

Quietly, I proceeded with my ablutions. I then asked my parents to sit side by side in a consecrated place and proceeded to circumambulate them. Having taken their blessings, I declared triumphantly, 'Give me my reward now, O Gauri, O Shankara, as I have accomplished the task you had set me.' Gravely, Shiva asked, 'How is that possible, my son?' I told him, 'What else is there in this universe but you? You, Shiva and Shakti, are the universe and I have circled you to complete my mission.' To my relief, I detected a smile on my father's lips and a look of immense pride in his eyes. The nervous gods, who had also gathered to witness the momentous contest, applauded my wisdom. Satisfied with my insight, my parents granted me not one but two wives—Riddhi and Siddhi—who represent success and prosperity.

But my real reward was the wisdom I attained. I understood and flowed in the beauty of my new-found enlightenment. But Skanda couldn't quite comprehend the gnosis of oneness that our parents represented. 'When Shiva and Parvati become one entity what happens to their other halves?' he wondered aloud. I told him, 'One was born on earth as Everyman, the other as Everywoman.' This is how the creator resides in each and every one of us and we become one with the universal spirit.It is so simple, after all. There is no need for elaborate rituals or arduous pilgrimages, just an understanding born of clear thinking that Shiva, along with Shakti, constitutes the whole universe and we are all representatives of this sublime truth.

Not much is known about the stages by which Ganesha came to be the popular deity he is today, but the cycle of myths connected with him indicates an evolutionary arc much like that of Shiva.

The Ganesha myths point to a complex process of interaction between the Vedic and non-Vedic worlds. While some scholars prefer to see Ganesha as a product of popular imagination, others believe he has been derived from the totem of a Dravidian tribe or some other pre-Vedic tradition. The worship of an elephant-headed deity probably commenced from the time when animals like the elephant and the bull were domesticated and assigned friendly, positive and participatory roles in human life and activities. Recognizing the power, majesty and usefulness of the physical qualities of these animals, tribal traditions incorporated them in the existing practice of totem worship and agrarian rites, perhaps out of fear of the elephant or the desire to acquire its strength. Eventually, the god associated with the animal was accorded the status of the guardian deity of the tribe. Such a process may be associated with the pre-Vedic traditions to which Rudra belonged, marking both Ganesha and Shiva as 'outsiders' to Vedic religion.

There is also a possibility that Ganesha evolved from the yaksha tradition. The discovery of an elephant-headed yaksha sculpture dating back to the second century CE in a temple in Amaravati reinforces this idea.[1] The yakshas, some of whom are depicted as being physically stunted, were worshipped to remove hindrances since it was believed that they possessed the power to plant difficulties in people's lives.

The idea of a Ganapati related to wisdom and learning, leadership and lordship, belongs to the Vedic tradition. The Ganapati of the Vedic sources is not the personal name of a god, it is a concept that has been variously applied to the Vedic god Brihaspati or Brahmanaspati, to Indra, and was later extended even to Rudra.[2] A similar case occurs with another well-known epithet of Ganesha, Vinayaka. Although in the Puranas Vinayaka is one of the names given to Ganesha, in the Atharvasiras Upanishad Vinayaka is among the many gods or spirits that Rudra is identified with. In the 'Anushasana Parva' of the Mahabharata, Ganeshwaras and Vinayakas are described along with other gods as the lords of the world who, when properly propitiated, remove obstacles from the path of men. It is clear that Ganapati and Vinayaka were at one point generic names, and the Ganesha we hear of later may have grown from them, incorporating their ideas and features. Dharmasutra texts also mention a class of beings called Vinayakas who possess people and require ritual propitiation. None of these are described as being elephant-headed, but they are spoken of as creating impediments.[3] In fact, the Vedic Ganapati has no clear-cut connection with the Puranic Ganesha who asserts the relationship between Shiva and Parvati.

Ganesha is also represented as a master of the arts and depicted in much of iconography in a graceful dancing pose. In this form he is called Nritya Ganapati. The Nritya Ganapati form was apparently invented in northern India in the sixth century. It spread throughout the subcontinent, becoming popular in Tibet and Nepal, but not in South-East Asia. The Nritya Ganapati seems to have inherited his talent for dance from his father. Though Shiva's is the many-splendoured dance of cosmic creation and dissolution, as the leader of Shiva's celestial attendants Ganesha dances in light-hearted, playful movements.

The imagery for the dancing Ganesha comes primarily from art, not from texts. In Cave No. 6 in Udayagiri, Madhya Pradesh, we see Ganesha joining the saptamatrikas in a dance celebrating Durga's destruction of Mahishasura. Ganesha is placed at the end of the panel, after the figures of the saptamatrikas. The matrikas' role in Hinduism is complex and Ganesha's association with them has surprised many. A possible explanation for this is that the goddesses and Ganesha were in the process of being adopted into mainstream Hinduism and as such were undergoing a very similar course of transformation from predominantly malevolent to generally benevolent deities. Many a malevolent deity has undergone centuries of 'culturization' and propitiation to be mellowed and thus made fit to be incorporated into the Hindu pantheon. Ganesha too has evolved from being Vijna, the one who creates obstacles, to a kind, generous, jovial god who is also a provider of wealth. Perhaps because the term 'Ganapati' was used to refer to Brihaspati, the lord of prayers and the patron of sages and wise men, Ganesha was subsequently endowed with the double reputation for wisdom and wealth, which made him one of the most popular deities among scholars as well as those interested in worldly prosperity. It may also be that an independent cult of worshipping an elephant-headed god was assimilated into Shaiva mythology—much like Nandi, Shiva's vahana, who was worshipped by himself as a bull among the Neolithic people at least a couple of thousand years before he was syncretized.

Thus, like his father, who was originally an outsider in the Hindu pantheon and in opposition to it, Ganesha stands at the threshold of the divine world. His residual attachment to the autochthonous, non-Vedic stream is evident in his iconography and mythology and in his entrance into the Shaiva pantheon as a legitimate god. In the latter role he dictates the Mahabharata to Vyasa and, of course, has to be worshipped before any 'higher' god.

Philosophically, Ganesha's elephant head is seen as signifying the macrocosm, the universe, and his body the microcosm, the individual. In other words the half-elephant half-human form stands for the cosmic and human dimensions of the world.

Sticky Births

Most Hindu gods present themselves to us wrapped in layers of myths. Ganesha's birth stories speak of an elemental lineage. In most of the tellings of Ganesha's birth Parvati creates him unilaterally. Shiva, the eternally living god, does not need a shradh ceremony to be performed by a son. He is also the Mahayogi and must retain his seed, which empowers him. He therefore does not feel the need to produce offspring.

One version of the story tells us about the repeated arguments between Shiva and Parvati over Parvati's desire for a child. She tells Shiva that he can return to his yoga once she has begotten a child secure in the knowledge that she will take care of their son on her own. She even assures him that if he so wishes his son will be averse to marriage, so a lineage will not be established. Shiva, angry at her nagging, pulls at her red sari and says, 'Now make a son of that and kiss it.' Parvati is hurt, but she takes the cloth and plays with it as though it were a child, swinging it in her arms and talking to it, pleading for it to come alive. And suddenly it does. (More often she rubs the dirt from her limbs and fashions it into a son.) She gives it her breast to suck and kisses the baby as he smiles at her.

Here, she plays the role of the male partner. Her bodily substance substitutes Shiva's seed and she creates Ganesha in a manner similar to the way Shiva created Skanda by casting his seed into the Ganga where it was nursed by the Krittikas. Nevertheless, since Shiva gives Ganesha a second life after beheading him, he enacts the role of the father, albeit in a meandering way. Both the deities benefit from this connection. Ganesha receives a pedigreed lineage and is acknowledged in the brahmanic pantheon as Shiva and Parvati's son and Shiva gains the added aspect of a thoroughbred householder, now that he is father to yet another son.

Ganapati

Ganesha's appointment as the head of the ganas is crucial when viewed in the context of Shiva's personal history.

In the Rig Veda Shiva as Rudra is associated with groups of semi-divine followers and troops such as the maruts and the rudras. The gana is a conceptual continuity of these godlings. A motley bunch of strange-faced creatures, alternately horrible and humorous, they act as guardians of the directions. In various myths Shiva's ganas are of supreme importance because they are constantly by his side and at his beck and call, following Shiva from place to place and carrying out his orders. They come to Shiva's aid during the destruction of Daksha's sacrifice, they accompany Sati on her lonely journey to her maternal home, they guard Kailash from intruders, or just enjoy roaming with Shiva and experiencing the bliss of being one with him. They draw their powers by being close to Shiva and later to Ganesha.

Shiva is Ashutosha, easy to please, and Bholanatha, the guileless one. In his eyes all creatures are equal and perfection does not lie in the physical, material being. Hence all sorts of creatures join his entourage and live in carefree bliss born of the non-conformity of their very beings. Many an autochthonous cult gets absorbed in this amorphous bunch where the only criteria seems to be the closeness to Shiva, as is found in the case of the saptamatrikas and the chaunsatha yoginis. It takes no effort on Shiva's part to be like them and he demonstrates this in his embodied form and through antinomian behaviour. Ganesha, too, with his strange physical features fits in well with the retinue. His many qualities of learning and wit, of art and dance, of cheerfulness and mischief, of tolerance and munificence, make him as popular among the 'weird' creatures who make up the ganas as he is among mortals on earth.

The Padma Purana contains a hymn which talks of Ganesha's physical characteristics being similar to Shiva's: 'Who has one tusk, whose body is big, who resembles heated gold, who has a large belly and large eyes, who has put on the munja (girdle) and the skin of a black antelope, and has the sacred thread of the serpents and on his head the digit of the young moon.'[4] There is also sculptural evidence of an Ardhanarishwara form of Ganesha. Though the accompanying myth is untraceable, it is a crucial index to the importance of similar traits manifested in Shiva and Ganesha.[5]

Oedipal Strain

There are endless ways in which devotees 'see' Ganesha. In recent years the myth surrounding the conflict between Shiva and Ganesha and the latter's subsequent death and restoration have tempted some scholars to introduce the theme of father–son aggression and invite comparisons with the myth of Oedipus. This has raised considerable controversy in academic as well as non-academic communities. I would look at it as an alternative way to view the symbolism behind the myth.

Freudian theory speaks of the son's childhood desire to bond with the mother and exclude the father. Ganesha standing on the threshold of Parvati's inner chambers is said to reflect this. Consequently, Shiva, the father, angry at being prevented from meeting his wife, mutilates his handsome son Ganesha. Hindu mythology contains many such parallel instances. Parashurama's father urges him to decapitate his mother.[6] Brahma destroys all of his sons. Indra gives a horse's head to Dadhyancha Dadhicha under similar circumstances.

Eventually, Shiva restores Ganesha's head, as he does for the other enemies he has decapitated. The act of beheading, however, is antagonistic, crucial in the context of the background myth of incest. Ganesha dwells on the threshold, like a mediator between Shiva and Parvati, as a source of both conflict and reconciliation, as children frequently do in the human world. Shiva has to go past Ganesha and overcome him—literally, as seen in the myths—in order to reach Parvati.

It is significant that even today Ganesha is the deity devotees must worship and pray to before they approach the inner shrine.

Bhakti and Advaita

The two myths in which Skanda and Ganesha interact underline the cornerstones of Hindu philosophy.

In the first, Ganesha identifies his parents as constituting the universe while Skanda takes the challenge before him quite literally and rushes off to conquer the physical universe. Shiva would have termed this 'avidya'. On the surface the incident between the two brothers Skanda and Ganesha may appear as sibling rivalry, but this myth directs the devotee to the appropriate mode of worship. The scriptures contain lengthy discussions on bhakti yoga, jnana yoga and karma yoga and different texts propagate different paths. Some lay emphasis on karma, others on both karma and bhakti. In the myth in question it is bhakti yoga that triumphs and devotion wins as the preferred path to salvation.

In the second, Ganesha answers Skanda's query regarding the Ardhanarishwara. Delightfully simple as Ganesha's response may seem, it carries the weight of advaitic philosophy behind it: 'Tat tvam asi', I am that. Every being is a representation of 'that', the universal spirit which allows one to feel complete and whole. There is no other but the Self here, and no pain of separation. With this realization the Self that each of us embodies experiences the lofty expansion of being one with the divine. Chidananda rupah Shivoham, Shivo'ham.

❧ Notes ❧

Introduction

1. All translations of verses from the Rig Veda are from Ralph T.H. Griffith (trans.), *The Hymns of the Rigveda*, Delhi: Motilal Banarsidass Publishers, 2004.

Vishnu

1. Catherine Jones, *Sex or Symbol: Erotic Images of Greece and Rome*, London: British Museum Publications, 1982.
2. Sri Sankaracarya, *Sivanandalahari*, Swami Tapasyananda (trans.), Madras: Sri Ramakrishna Math, 1985, verse 99.
3. Ibid., verse 23.
4. Ibid., verse 99.
5. Ralph T.H. Griffith (trans.), *The Hymns of the Rigveda*, Delhi: Motilal Banarsidass Publishers, 2004, 2.1.6.; Griffith (trans.), *The Hymns of the Atharvaveda*, Delhi: Motilal Banarsidass Publishers, 2004, 7.8.7.

6. T.M.P. Mahadevan, *The Hymns of Sankara*, Delhi: Motilal Banarsidass Publishers, 1980, 113.

7. Siva Purana, Ancient Indian Tradition and Mythology Series, Delhi: Motilal Banarsidass Publishers, 1969–70, 3.20.3–7.

8. Brahmanda Purana, Ancient Indian Tradition and Mythology Series, Delhi: Motilal Banarsidass Publishers, 1983, 2.4.34–76.

9. Radhika Sekar, *The Sabarimalai Pilgrimage and Ayyappan Cultus*, Delhi: Motilal Banarsidass Publishers, 1992, 28.

10. Nilima Chitgopekar, *Encountering Sivaism: The Deity, the Milieu, the Entourage*, Delhi: Munshiram Manoharlal Publishers, 1998, 123.

11. Ellen Goldberg, *The Lord Who is Half Woman: Ardhanarisvara in Indian and Feminist Perspective*, Albany: State University of New York Press, 2002, 53–55.

12. Sri Sankaracarya, *Sivanandalahari*, Swami Tapasyananda (trans.), Madras: Sri Ramakrishna Math, 1985, verse 82.

13. Partha Mitter, *Indian Art*, New Delhi: OUP, 2001, 37.

Sati

1. David Kinsley, *The Ten Mahavidyas: Tantric Visions of the Divine Feminine*, Delhi: Motilal Banarsidass Publishers, 2003, 25.

2. William Sax, cited in Kinsley, op.cit., 26–27.

Daksha

1. Griffith (trans.), *The Hymns of the Rigveda*, 10.136.

2. G.S. Ghurye, *Indian Sadhus*, Bombay: Popular Prakashan, 1953, 13.

3. Robert Lewis Gross, *The Sadhus of India: A Study of Hindu Asceticism*, New Delhi: Rawat Publications, 1992, 23.

Parvati

1. Siva Purana, 3.46.485.
2. Siva Purana, 4.1839, fn. 215.
3. Siva Purana, 2.61.589.
4. N.P. Joshi, *Tapasvini Parvati: Iconographic Study of Parvati in Penance*, Delhi: New Age International Publishers, 1996.
5. Goldberg, 142.
6. Siva Purana, 6.22.1–58.
7. Ajayagadh Rock Inscription of Kalyanadevi, *Epigraphia Indica*, vol. 1, 329.
8. Sri Sankaracarya, *Saundaryalahari*, Swami Tapasyananda (trans.), Madras: Sri Ramakrishna Math, 1987, 84.
9. Goldberg, 2.

Ganesha

1. Anita Raina Thapan, *Understanding Ganapati: Insights into the Dynamics of a Cult*, New Delhi: Manohar Publishers, 1997.
2. Debiprasad Chattopadhyaya, *Lokayata: A Study in Ancient Indian Materialism*, New Delhi: People's Publishing House, 1992, 128.
3. Paul B. Courtright, *Ganesa: Lord of Obstacles, Lord of Beginnings*, New York: OUP, 1985, 7.
4. Padma Purana, Ancient Indian Tradition and Mythology Series, Delhi: Motilal Banarsidass Publishers, 1991, 64. 2–3.
5. Chitgopekar, 144.
6. Varaha Purana, Ancient Indian Tradition and Mythology Series, Delhi: Motilal Banarsidass Publishers, 1985, 23.16–19.

Bibliography

Primary Sources

The Agni Purana, Parts I–II, Ancient Indian Tradition and Mythology Series (AITM Series), 1986.

The Bhagavat Purana, Parts I–III, AITM Series, Delhi: Motilal Banarsidass Publishers, 1976.

The Brahmanda Purana, Parts I–II, AITM Series, Delhi: Motilal Banarsidass Publishers, 1983.

Brihadaranyaka Upanishad, Swami Madhavananda (trans.), Calcutta: Advaita Ashrama, 1993.

Chhandogya Upanishad, Swami Gambhirananda (trans.), Calcutta: Advaita Ashrama, 1993.

Eight Upanishads (Aitareya, Mundaka, Mandukya and Karika, Prasna, Isa, Kena, Katha, Taittiriya), 2 vols, Swami Gambhirananda (trans.), Calcutta: Advaita Ashrama, 1992.

Epigraphia Indica, Vol. 1., Delhi: Archaeological Survey of India, 1892.

The Kurma Purana, Parts I–II, AITM Series, Delhi: Motilal Banarsidass Publishers, 1982–83.

The Linga Purana, Parts I–II, AITM Series, Delhi: Motilal Banarsidass Publishers, 1973.

The Padma Purana, Parts I–IX, AITM Series, Delhi: Motilal Banarsidass Publishers, 1991.

Ralph T.H. Griffith (trans.), *The Hymns of the Rigveda*, Delhi: Motilal Banarsidass Publishers, 2004.

_____ (trans.), *The Hymns of the Atharvaveda,* Delhi: Motilal Banarsidass Publishers, 2004.

The Siva Purana, Parts I–IV, AITM Series, Delhi: Motilal Banarsidass Publishers, 1969–70.

The Skanda Purana, Parts I–IV, AITM Series, Delhi: Motilal Banarsidass Publishers, 1992–94.

Sri Sankaracarya, *Saundaryalahari*, Swami Tapasyananda (trans.), Madras: Sri Ramakrishna Math, 1987.

Sri Sankaracarya, *Sivanandalahari*, Swami Tapasyananda (trans.), Madras: Sri Ramakrishna Math, 1985.

Swami Gambhirananda (trans.), Shvetashvatara Upanishad, Calcutta: Advaita Ashrama, 1986.

T.M.P. Mahadevan, *The Hymns of Sankara*, Delhi: Motilal Banarsidass Publishers, 1980.

The Varaha Purana, Parts I–IV, AITM Series, Delhi: Motilal Banarsidass Publishers, 1985.

The Vayu Purana, Part I, AITM Series, Delhi: Motilal Banarsidass Publishers, 1987.

Secondary Readings

A.K. Ramanujan (trans.), *Speaking of Siva*, New Delhi: Penguin Books India, 1992.

Aditya Malik, Anne Feldhaus and Heldrun Bruckner, *In the Company of Gods*, Delhi: Manohar Publishers, 2005.

Aghenanda Bharati, *The Tantric Tradition,* London: Rider & Company, 1965.

Alain Danielou, *Hindu Polytheism*, USA: Pantheon Books, 1964.

Ananda K. Coomaraswamy, *Hinduism and Buddhism*, New York: The Philosophical Library, 1960.

Anita Raina Thapan, *Understanding Ganapati: Insights into the Dynamics of a Cult,* New Delhi: Manohar Publishers, 1997.

Ashis Nandy, *At the Edge of Psychology: Essays in Politics and Culture*, Delhi: OUP, 1980.

_____, *Time Warps in the Insistent Politics of Silent and Evasive Pasts,* New Delhi: Permanent Black, 2001.

Catherine Jones, *Sex or Symbol: Erotic Images of Greece and Rome*, London: British Museum Publications, 1982.

D.C. Sircar, *Studies in the Religious Life of Ancient and Medieval India,* Delhi: Motilal Banarsidass, 1971.

David R. Kinsley, *Hindu Goddesses: Vision of the Divine Feminine in the Hindu Religious Tradition,* Delhi: Motilal Banarsidass Publishers, 1987.

_____, *The Ten Mahavidyas: Tantric Visions of the Divine Feminine*, Delhi: Motilal Banarsidass Publishers, 2003.

Debiprasad Chattopadhyaya, *Indian Philosophy: A Popular Introduction*, New Delhi: People's Publishing House, 1986.

_____, *Lokayata: A Study in Ancient Indian Materialism,* New Delhi: People's Publishing House, 1992.

Devdutt Pattanaik, *Indian Mythology: Tales, Symbols and Rituals from the Heart of the Subcontinent,* India: Inner Traditions, 2003.

Elizabeth De Michelis, *A History of Modern Yoga*, London: Continuum, 2004.

Ellen Goldberg, *The Lord Who is Half Woman: Ardhanarisvara in Indian and Feminist Perspective*, Albany: State University of New York Press, 2002.

Eustace Haydon, *Biography of the Gods*, New York: Frederick Ungar Publishing Co., 1941.

Francis X. Clooney, *Hindu Wisdom for All God's Children*, New York: Orbis Books, 1998.

Gail Hinich Sutherland, *Yaksa in Hinduism and Buddhism: The Disguises of the Demon*, Delhi: Manohar Publishers, 1992.

Gavin Flood, *An Introduction to Hinduism*, UK: Cambridge University Press, 1996.

Haripada Chakroborti, *Pasupata Sutram*, Calcutta: Academie Publishers, 1970.

Heinrich Zimmer, *Myths and Symbols in Indian Art and Civilization*, Bollingen Foundation, 1972.

_____, *The Art of Indian Asia*, vol.1, Delhi: Motilal Banarsidass Publishers, 1984.

Herman Oldenberg, *The Doctrine of the Upanishads and the Early Buddhism* (trans. Shridhar B. Shrotri), Delhi: Motilal Banarsidass Publishers, 1991.

J.N. Mohanty, *Classical Indian Philosophy*, Delhi: OUP, 2002.

J.N. Banerjea, *Pauranic and Tantric Religion (Early Phase)*, Calcutta: University of Calcutta, 1966.

_____, *Religion in Art and Archaeology (Vaishnavism and Saivism)*, Lucknow: University of Lucknow, 1968.

Jeaneane Fowler, *Perspectives of Reality: An Introduction to the Philosophy of Hinduism*, Brighton: Sussex Academic Press, 2002.

John R. Hinnells, ed., *The Routledge Companion to the Study of Religion*, UK: Routledge, 2005.

June McDaniel, *The Madness of the Saints: Ecstatic Religion in Bengal*, Chicago: University of Chicago Press, 1989.

K.M. Sen, *Hinduism*, London: Penguin Books, 2005.

Laurie L. Patton, *Bringing the Gods to Mind: Mantra and Ritual in Early Indian Sacrifice*, USA: University of California Press, 2005.

M.G. Bhagat, *Ancient Indian Asceticism*, Delhi: Munshiram Manoharlal Publishers, 1976.

Michael W. Meister, *Discourses on Siva*, Philadelphia: University of Pennsylvania, 1984.

Mircea Eliade, *Essential Sacred Writings from around the World*, San Francisco: Harper, 1977.

N.N. Bhattacharyya, *The Indian Mother Goddess*, reprint, New Delhi: Manohar Publishers, 1999.

——, *History of the Tantric Religion*, Delhi: Manohar Publishers, 1992.

——, *Indian Religious Historiography*, Delhi: Munshiram Manoharlal Publishers, 1996.

N.P. Joshi, *Tapasvini Parvati: Iconographic Study of Parvati in Penance*, Delhi: New Age International Publishers, 1996.

Nilima Chitgopekar, *Encountering Sivaism: The Deity, the Milieu, the Entourage*, Delhi: Munshiram Manoharlal, 1998.

——, ed., *Invoking Goddesses: Gender Politics in Indian Religion*, Delhi: Har-Anand Publishers, 2002.

Patrick Olivelle, *The Asrama System: The History and Hermeneutics of a Religious Institution*, US: OUP, 1993.

Paul B. Courtright, *Ganesa: Lord of Obstacles, Lord of Beginnings*, New York: OUP, 1985.

Paul Bowen, ed., *Themes and Issues in Hinduism*, London: Cassell, 1998.

Peter Heehs, ed., *Indian Religions: The Spiritual Traditions of South Asia*, Delhi: Permanent Black, 2002.

R.N. Dandekar, *Vedic Mythological Tracts*, Delhi: Ajanta Publications, 1979.

Rachel Fell McDermott and Jeffrey J. Kripal, *Encountering Kali: In the Margins, at the Center, in the West*, USA: University of California Press, 2003.

Robert Lewis Gross, *The Sadhus of India: A Study of Hindu Asceticism*, New Delhi: Rawat Publications, 1992.

S.A. Dange, *Glimpses of Puranic Myth and Culture*, Delhi: Ajanta Publications, 1987.

Sabyasachi Bhattacharya, Sarvepalli Gopal and Romila Thapar, eds., *Situating Indian History*, New Delhi: OUP, 1986.

Sarah Strauss, *Positioning Yoga: Balancing Acts across Cultures*, Oxford: Berg, 2005.

Seemanthini Niranjana, *Gender and Space: Femininity and Sexualization and the Female Body*, New Delhi: Sage Publications, 2001.

Sitakant Mahapatra, ed., *The Realm of the Sacred: Verbal Symbolism and Ritual Structures*, New York: OUP, 1992.

Sri Aurobindo, *The Foundations of Indian Culture*, Pondicherry: Sri Aurobindo Ashram, 1998.

Stanley Kurtz, *All the Mothers Are One: Hindu India and the Cultural Reshaping of Psychoanalysis*, USA: Columbia University Press, 1992.

Sudhir Kakar, *Culture and Psyche: Selected Essays*, Delhi: OUP, 1997.

———, *The Inner World: A Psychoanalytic Study of Childhood and Society in India*, Delhi: OUP, 1978.

Sukumari Bhattacharji, *The Indian Theogony*, Delhi: Motilal Banarsidass Publishers, 1970.

Susan Frank Parsons, *The Ethics of Gender*, USA: Blackwell Publishers, 2001.

Sushil Mittal and Gene Thursby, eds., *The Hindu World*, UK: Routledge, 2004.

T.S. Maxwell, *The Gods of Asia: Image Text and Meaning*, New Delhi: OUP, 1997.

Thomas A. Forsthoefel, *Knowing Beyond Knowledge: Epistemologies of Religious Experience in Classical and Modern Advaita*, USA: Ashgate, 2002.

Thorkil Vangaard, *Phallos: A Symbol and Its History in the Male World*, London: Jonathan Cape, 1969.

Tracy Pintchman, *The Rise of the Goddess in the Hindu Tradition*, Albany: State University of New York Press, 1994.

V.S. Pathak, *Saiva Cults in North India, from Inscriptions 700 AD to 1200 AD*, Varanasi, 1960.

V.S. Agrawal, *Ancient Indian Folk Cults*, Varanasi: Prithvi Prakashan, 1970.

Vidya Dehejia, *Indian Art*, London: Phaidon Press Ltd, 1997.

Wendy Doniger O'Flaherty, *Sexual Metaphors and Animal Symbols in Indian Mythology*, Chicago: University of Chicago Press, 1980.

_____, *Sexual Metaphors and Animal Symbols in Indian Mythology*, Delhi: Motilal Banarsidass Publishers, 1980.

_____, *Siva: The Erotic Ascetic*, Delhi: OUP, 1973.

_____ (trans.), *Hindu Myths: A Sourcebook*, London: Penguin Books, 1975.

W.J. Wilkins, *Hindu Mythology (Vedic and Puranic)*, New Delhi: The Delhi Bookstore, 1972.

Yohanan Grinshpon, *Crisis and Knowledge: The Upanishadic Experience of Storytelling*, Delhi: OUP, 2003.

❀❀❀ Acknowledgements ❀❀❀

I am grateful to Ravi Singh of Penguin India for the unfussy suggestion that such a book would be possible. It was more than pleasant working with Poulomi Chatterjee, whose keenness in the subject often went beyond editorial fundamentals. The Charles Wallace India Trust facilitated a visit to the UK, where, besides other resources, I was able to benefit from the interaction with other scholars working in the field of Hinduism.